Echoes of Hope

A Comprehensive Bible Study on Faith's Resilience - Delving Deep into Bible Stories for Modern Serenity and Spiritual Strength

Lucas Andrew Bennett

ISBN : 9798860639737

Table of Contents

1

Introduction

1.1 Setting the Context: Why Bible Stories Matter

The Bible, as one of the oldest written records of human spirituality and thought, offers an incredible wellspring of wisdom, history, and insight. At first glance, these narratives may seem distant from our modern lives; however, through a closer look and careful interpretation, we can find resonating messages that still hold relevance in our daily existence. As we step into the vast landscape of Biblical narratives, it's essential to remember that these stories were born out of specific cultural and historic contexts. Each tale was written against a backdrop of particular social norms, historical happenings and theological perspectives of the time. This added layer of understanding will allow us to delve much deeper into the underlying messages and themes communicated through these ancient words.

Take, for example, the familiar tale of David and Goliath. Often, we focus on the miracle of David's victory, a mere shepherd boy defeating a giant, forgetting the context in which this event occurred. At its core, this event reflects not just an individual's triumph but a revelation about the power of faith and courage against all odds. The story is not merely about physical might but the strength of spiritual resilience and faith in God. Similar cultural and historical subtleties imbue the narrative of Moses leading the Israelites out of Egypt. On a surface level, it serves as a powerful story of liberation from slavery. However, when we factor in the social and political situations of that era, the story's depth is revealed. It becomes a tale of hope and faith, a reflection of resilience against oppressive power structures - something that resonates with struggles for freedom and justice throughout human history.

Remember when Jesus interacted with the woman at the well in the book of John's account? The mere act of engaging with a Samaritan woman, in public, was laden with implications due to the strict social norms of the day. If we disregard this context, we miss the groundbreaking nature of Jesus' actions and his teachings on love, equality, and acceptance. Engaging with Scripture in such a manner invites a dynamic and profound exploration of the Bible. It involves understanding the historical implications, acknowledging cultural nuances and drawing upon these to interpret how God's word speaks to us today.

Let's briefly outline the processes involved in understanding the cultural and historic significance of Biblical narratives:

1. Familiarize yourself with the historical and cultural context: Research the prevailing societal norms, belief systems, and historical events of the time. Keep in mind that the Bible encompasses a span of several centuries, and society's many shifts and changes in that time can impact our understanding of the stories.
2. Analyze the text: Reflect on the narrative in light of your understanding of the historical and socio-cultural context.
3. Connect to modern times: Contemplate how the themes and messages of these stories resonate in today's societal context. Distinguish between timeless truths and cultural specifics.
4. Apply personally: Reflect on how these messages resonate with your own life and spiritual journey.

Wading through these ancient narratives with this approach, we will find that the echoes of hope, tales of faith's resilience, and lessons of serenity and spiritual strength reverberate from the Bible's pages, across centuries, and land in the heart of our modern lives. Anchor your heart with astounding truth and undeniable wisdom as we delve into stories nestled within the Old Testament. Biblical parables etch on the sands of time, unchanging and profound, waiting to be deciphered, adapted, and applied to our lives.

Firstly, set sight on the story of Joseph. Sold into slavery by his envious brothers, he endured treachery and deceit but maintained steadfast in his faith. The key lesson is the unwavering resilience Joseph demonstrated in the face of adversity and despair. This resilience spoke of faith, fortitude, and forgiveness. A modern interpretation of this parable could be: no matter the trials we face, cultivating a heart of forgiveness, bound steadfast in faith, might lead us to greater blessings.

Proceeding ahead, contemplate on the tale of Jonah and the whale. The narrative is complex, weaving themes of civil disobedience, repentance, and divine grace fervently. The profound wisdom within this parable reminds us of the imperative necessity of obedience to divine guidance and the boundless grace that accommodates countless repentance. In our current lives, this story espouses the magnanimity of forgiving ourselves and others while reaffirming our faith's resilience.

Moreover, the sagas of patriarchs like Abraham echo the virtues of obedience to divine will and the audacious resilience of belief. Despite his age and seemingly impossible circumstances, Abraham's faith never faltered, becoming a beacon of hope and perseverance for all who feel overwhelmed by life's challenges.

Turning to the stories of Moses, we can draw lessons on resilience, leadership, and faith. Despite facing severe adversities, Moses led his people out of Egypt into the promised land, guided by his unwavering trust in the divine. His story serves to illuminate unwavering faith – an enduring belief in divine guidance – can lead us through the harshest trials to a destination of serenity and spiritual strength.

Glean insight from the life of King David, too. Despite his struggles with human flaws, he reigned with justice, faith, and compassion. David's life is a testament to the truth that spiritual strength is not exempt from weakness, but it indeed thrives despite it. His resilience should serve as a beacon for all of us managing our fallibility, nudging us toward forgiveness and wisdom.

Finally, the parable of Daniel in the lions' den serves as an emblematic testimony of unwavering faith. In the face of perilous adversity, Daniel valued his relationship with the divine to the point of choosing a lion's den over compromise. His tale nurtures the seeds of faith's invincibility, provoking us to redefine our understanding of courage and spiritual resilience.

In conclusion, the parables of the Old Testament serve as visual metaphors guiding the journey toward modern serenity and spiritual strength. The inherent wisdom submerged beneath these narratives kindles the flame of resilience, illuminating our path forward with tales of courage, obedience, and steadfast faith. As we decode and absorb these lessons, we will find ourselves in a space that celebrates spiritual strength and cultivates a serene atmosphere for growth and redemption.

Story Title	Main Theme	Message
Creation Story	God's Power	The Beginning of Everything
The Fall of Adam and Eve	Loss of Innocence	Consequences of Disobedience
The Flood and Noah's Ark	God's Judgment and Mercy	Survival and Promise
Tower of Babel	Human ambition	Understanding Diversity
Abraham's Covenant	Trust in God	God's faithfulness
Moses and the Exodus	Liberty	Freedom from Bondage

In our examination, one cannot overlook the undying influence of these ancient tales on our modern perceptions of faith and resilience. The stories told and retold throughout the generations don't merely communicate historical happenings; they pull upon resounding themes of struggle, survival, hope, and the human capacity to adapt in the face of adversity. A striking example is the account of Job, a righteous man who befalls an array of trials. He loses his wealth, health, and children, almost all the worldly things he prized. But through the ashes of despair, Job arrives at a profound understanding about the divine plan beyond human comprehension. His story continues to inspire people today, reminding them of the potential to retain faith amid life's often brutal trials.

No less significant is the narrative of Moses leading the Israelites out of Egypt towards the Promised Land. It symbolizes hope, liberation, and the human ability to withstand grueling circumstances for an anticipated brighter future. It resonates deeply with those grappling with struggles, offering them a beacon of hope for future freedom and contentment. The tale of the Prodigal Son, too, echoes the universal mantra of remorse, forgiveness, and redemption that has survived the passage of time. This story continues to provide comfort and solace to many seeking spiritual fortitude, affirming that it is never too late to turn away from past misdeeds and regain a rightful place with God. Moreover, the parable of the Good Samaritan retains great relevance, even in our present society, filled with ethnic and religious conflicts. It encapsulates the encouragement to love one's enemy, extending kindness without discrimination or prejudice. This divine principle still echoes in our world today, advocating peace, unity, and the enduring power of empathy.

The biblical tale of Daniel in the lion's den illustrates faith's resilience against seemingly insurmountable odds. This narrative's resonance in our hearts and minds fosters a never-ending testament to the strength of resolves anchored in unshakeable faith. Daniel's story is a tale of hope triumphant, flaring brightly in the dense darkness of fear and improbability. Finally, the journey of Esther, a vibrant figure of courage and faith, offers a stirring reminder of the power of prayer and fasting. In the face of imminent annihilation of her people, Esther does not cower. Instead, she turns to structured spiritual practices to draw strength and wisdom. Esteemed in the Bible as an epitome of bravery, she remains a beacon of faith's resilience for many even to this day. Each of these narratives, and the many we cannot delve into due to the limits of space, serve as timeless reminders of human spirit's resilience and the potent influence of faith within us. They infuse contemporary conversations with spiritual fortitude, sometimes offering necessary perspectives to navigate through life's rough terrains. In the dense layers of their teachings lay the keys to maintaining spiritual strength, the means to seek serenity, and the echoes of an ageless hope. Regardless of evolving cultural or societal norms, these Bible narratives continue to shape our shared understandings and dialogues around resilience, spirituality, and faith.

Journal Exercise:

Pause for a moment and consider your understanding of Bible stories prior to this chapter. In your journal, write down why you think these stories hold significance. After engaging with the chapter, do you see them in a different light? Share your thoughts. Reflect on a specific Bible story that resonates with you and how it applies to your current life situation. How do you feel this narrative encourages resilience in your faith journey? Make note of any questions or topics you'd like to delve deeper into as you continue this study.

1.2 The Power of Resilient Faith

When we think of how faith and resilience intertwine, we often think about how the Bible has shed light on this correlation through several stories of individuals navigating through their own tribulations. These accounts pave the way for modern understanding of how faith could be an anchor during the stormier times of life. Consider the story of Joseph, son of Jacob. Joseph was sold into slavery by his brothers due to jealousy, and this misfortune placed him in Egypt, far away from his family and the familiar. Yet, his faith in God never wavered. Joseph knew that God had a plan for him, and despite the strange path it was taking, he trusted in the Lord. This resilience borne of faith led to his eventual rise as one of Pharaoh's most trusted advisors.

Another compelling episode is the tale of Job, who was tested to the limits. By losing his family, his health, and his prosperity, Job had every reason to abandon faith. But he clung to his beliefs, regardless of his severe trials. His resilience was rewarded, as God restored his prosperity twofold.

David, the shepherd boy turned king, faced several adversities including the threat to his life by a jealous King Saul. Yet, he continued to have faith in God who had anointed him. His psalms are a testament to his steadfast faith in the face of adversity – his words ring true to this day as a source of comfort during times of distress. Consider also the case of Daniel, a young man taken captive by a hostile nation. Despite this, his faith in God was undeterred. His loyalty to his beliefs even in the face of life-threatening situations is a prime example of spiritual resilience.

Time and time again, the Bible is infused with narratives that highlight the resilience of faith during trials. These historical accounts are no mere stories, but practical examples of faith in action amid life's storms. The protagonists in these events were real individuals, facing very realistic hardships. As we delve deeper into these biblical instances, we can draw parallels, find comfort, learn resilience, and glean wisdom for our own individual journeys of faith. By exploring these stories, we learn that irrespective of our circumstance, faith can serve as our beacon amidst the turmoil, our steadfast companion that refuses to yield under pressure. To understand faith as a source of spiritual strength, it's beneficial to delve into the lives of key figures in the Bible who exhibited extraordinary faith in times of adversity. To see and comprehend their faith is to understand the 'anchors in the tides'; sturdy, unshakeable beliefs that have remained resilient throughout the passage of time.

The first person to consider is Abraham. His faith was manifest in his willingness to leave his homeland and journey into the unknown, purely based on God's promise. He firmly believed that God would guide him and his descendants into a promised land - a land flowing with milk and honey.

His unflinching faith enabled him to overcome every hurdle he faced in his journey, and because of this, he is hailed as the 'Father of Faith.'

Secondly, we see extraordinary faith demonstrated by the shunammite woman in the books of Kings. Even when her son died, she did not waver but clung onto the belief that Prophet Elisha could resurrect him. Her faith was unwavering, even in the face of immense adversity, which provides an excellent example for us in modern contexts.

The Apostle Paul is another figure to observe. Despite multiple imprisonments, beatings, and shipwrecks, Paul never sacrificed his faith. Instead, he held on tighter, professing the name of Jesus even in the darkest of times. His faith in Christ was his anchor, his source of strength, which allowed him to endure hardships and still spread the word of God.

In these biblical accounts, we see faith acting as an anchor, holding the individuals steady in times of hardship. This metaphorical anchor doesn't nullify the storm, but it does provide stability amid the rolling waves, enabling the believer to hold on until the storm passes. The dissection of these narratives equips us with a valuable lesson - our faith can be a powerful source of spiritual strength, acting as an anchor during life's tempests. Just like Abraham, the Shunammite woman, and Paul, we can trust in God's promises and providence, finding stability and serenity in our faith. In essence, the 'anchors in the tides' serve as a testament to the power of faith - it bolsters us when we're weak, gives us courage when we're afraid, and offers comfort when we're in pain. But, it's up to us to tether our faith tightly and hold on, regardless of the intensity of the storms we face.

We must remember:

- Faith is not a mere belief; it's a conviction that guides our thoughts, actions, and decisions.
- Faith should remain steadfast, even when circumstances seek to break it.
- With faith as our anchor, we can weather any storm with resilience and grace.
- The manifestation of spiritual strength through unwavering faith is a biblical principle that is just as applicable in modern times.

Diving into these stories from the Bible, there lies the potential to uncover not only a deeper understanding of faith itself but a practical application of these principles aimed at maintaining modern serenity and spiritual strength amidst life's uncertainties. It's in comprehending these facets of faith that we can find peace and fulfillment, drawing on the profound strength that faith provides.

Key Concepts	Related Scriptures	Personal Reflections
Trust in adversity	Psalm 46:1-3	How can I demonstrate trust even in trouble?
Endurance	James 1:2-4	What situations am I currently enduring and how?
Hope	Hebrews 11:1	How is faith the evidence of things not seen?
Strength in weakness	2 Corinthians 12:9-11	How can my weaknesses become a strength?
Peace in chaos	John 14:27	How can I maintain peace in chaotic situations?
Unwavering faith	James 1:6	How can I cultivate an unwavering faith?

There is tremendous power in the echoes of biblical truths that can be harnessed in our modern life. Let us begin by exploring how to apply the principles of resilient faith to build strength and peace in our daily lives. To create an enduring faith, it is essential that we first appreciate the intrinsic quality of resilience itself. In the Bible, resilience isn't about escaping suffering, but rather how one endures and grows from it. The Apostle Paul, for example, experienced numerous adversities yet he remained undeterred. He stated in Romans 5:3-4, "we also glory in our sufferings, because we know that suffering produces perseverance; perseverance, character; and character, hope." It is this sort of transformative resilience that we should strive to emulate.

Here are seven steps to assist in applying biblical principles of resilient faith in our modern life:

- Learn to Embrace Change: Life is full of change. Understand the nature of impermanence and find ways to appreciate the transformation and growth it brings. Use the account of Abraham, who left his homeland without knowing where he was going, as an example of adaptability.

- ❖ Practice Humility: An inflated ego brings stress and scars relationships. The Bible calls for humility. As Philippians 2:3 advises, "do nothing out of selfish ambition or vain conceit. Rather, in humility value others above yourselves."
- ❖ Be Forgiving: Jesus on the cross asked for forgiveness for those who brutalized and killed him. If He can forgive, so must we. Resilience often means releasing old hurts to create a space for growth and healing.
- ❖ Cultivate Inner Strength: Just as David relied on his trust in God to face Goliath, so should we cultivate an inner resilience that isn't reliant on our outward circumstances.
- ❖ Keep Hope Alive: Remember the hope-filled message of the resurrection - that even in the darkest hours, there can be a new beginning. Suffering is temporary but hope is eternal.
- ❖ Stay Connected to Others: The early Christians formed close-knit communities. To foster resilience, build a network of supportive relationships.
- ❖ Stay Connected to God: Above all, faith produces resilience through a deep-rooted connection with God. Stay in constant communion with Him through prayer and His Word.

Remember, it is not the strength of your storms that determines your ability to survive; it is the strength of your anchor. And your anchor is your faith. Look for ways to apply these principles in your everyday life and let the echoes of God's resilient hope ring loud in your heart. As we move forward on our spiritual journey, may we carry with us the wisdom of resilient faith, and may we return, constantly and consistently, to the foundations of our belief. Not to reiterate old pains, but to recognize the strength we have since cultivated. With each echo of hope, may our faith grow stronger, our hearts more resilient, and our spirits brimming with divine serenity.

Journal Exercise:

1. Begin by reflecting on a time when you had to rely heavily on your faith. Write about how it felt, the challenge(s) you faced, and how your faith helped you through that time.
2. Consider the chapter's discussion of resilience in faith. Choose a character from the Bible that exemplifies this resilience for you. Note down the character's story, the hardships they faced and how they used their faith to persevere.

3. Now, apply this Bible story to your own life - are there areas where you need more resilience in your faith? Make a commitment here about what steps you can take to build up this resilience.
4. Finish by writing a short prayer, asking for resilience and strength from God in the face of your own struggles and thanking Him for the lessons learned through His Word.

1.3 Reader's Guide: How to Navigate This Study

As we reflect upon the wisdom of the Bible, we find lessons prepared for every ear - for those in the midst of storms and for the ones enjoying calm waters. But to truly perceive the messages within, one needs to have 'ears to hear,' an open mind and heart ready to receive and embrace wisdom. To understand the perspective of biblical characters and the lessons embedded in their narratives, a clear understanding of certain key biblical themes is necessary.

- Faith: This is not merely a belief, but a complete trust or confidence in God's promises, even when circumstances suggest otherwise. We see such unwavering faith in the life of Abraham who was ready to sacrifice his son Isaac, fully trusting God's promise.
- Mercy: Often, stories in the Bible exemplify God's unending mercy. Despite human failings, God remains merciful. A perfect portrayal of this is found in the Parable of the Prodigal Son, where upon the son's return, the father shows unconditional mercy.
- Redemption: The theme of redemption is seen in almost every Bible story. It is ultimately about being freed from guilt, shame, and the power of sin. The story of Jesus Christ's sacrifice is the ultimate narrative of redemption.
- Reverence: The Bible teaches the importance of fostering a reverence or deep respect for God. Moses removing his sandals before the burning bush exemplifies this deep reverence, acknowledging the sanctity of God's presence.
- Resilience: Many of the Bible's best-known stories highlight resilience in the face of adversity and hardship. Job's story is a resounding testament to this, highlighting how unwavering faith can help us withstand life's tests.
- Love: God's agape, or selfless love, is central to the biblical message. This is most profoundly demonstrated by Christ's crucifixion, a sacrifice of love for humanity.

Understanding these concepts enriches our study of Bible stories, allowing us to perceive the profound messages woven into each narrative. These themes provide key lenses through which to examine the lives of biblical figures and extract wisdom applicable to our present day lives. In developing 'ears to hear,' we must remain open to the truths echoing within the centuries-old narratives of the Bible. We must turn our attention inward, tuning out external noise and distractions to fully absorb, understand, and embody the lessons within. This is a crucial step in transforming our Bible study from a mere intellectual exercise to a truly enriching spiritual journey.

Reflecting on biblical narratives is more than a surface level reading; it necessitates delving into the profound depths of texts that contain layers of meanings. As you explore, consider employing these interpretative strategies to gain a deeper insight into these sacred texts:

- Apply Contextual Analysis: Context is critical in interpreting any text, more so with the Bible. Understand the historical, cultural, and societal setting of a story to grasp its true significance. Realize the conditions, practices, and beliefs during the era the verses were written.
- Consider the Literary Structure: Each book of the Bible is an intricate literary masterpiece. Understanding the designated structure, be it historical documentation, wisdom literature, or poetic verses, assists in comprehending its message. Look for recurring themes, repetition of phrases, and symbols to detect underlying motifs.
- Interpret Symbols and Figures: Biblical narratives are rich with symbolic language and figures of speech. Knowing to identify these and understanding what they represent in the given cultural and historical context enriches the reading experience.
- Cross-Referencing: Scripture often interprets scripture. Make connections between different biblical texts which speak on similar topics. This comparative study can provide profound insights, clarify doubts and layer your understanding.
- Refer to Reputable Commentaries: Insight from renowned biblical scholars can add depth to your understanding and help unravel complex passages.
- Pray: Prayer is an indispensable part of Bible study. Ask for divine guidance to enlighten you, to help you to not just read but understand and live the Word.

Besides, it is also essential to be patient with oneself. Knowledge and wisdom from the Bible come with time and perseverance. Just as a seed slowly sprouts and blossoms into a beautiful plant, so will your understanding of the holy text grow and bear spiritual fruits. Remember, the golden threads of wisdom woven into these narratives span centuries and cultures. They breathe love and life into our everyday existence.

There might be times when certain narratives unsettle you, or when you find a passage difficult to interpret or accept, but do not discourage. Instead, take them as opportunities for growth. Try to see what they tell you about your own belief system, your prejudices, or preconceived notions. You may be surprised at the transformation this leads to, the shift in perspective, the enhanced spiritual strength, and the serenity it gifts. Always remember, each passage, each story in the Bible is a direct dialogue between God and you, filled with potent messages awaiting to be discovered, pondered, and lived.

In our present times, challenges are inevitable, from health crises to financial constraints, and emotional strain to societal pressures. Bridging the gap between the echoed stories of the sacred text and our modern dilemmas may seem daunting. However, the wisdom of these ancient words still pulsate with living guidance, offering practical solutions when we take time to properly reflect and apply. In the Bible, we see how different individuals faced and transcended adversities. There are significant principles to learn from these stories when we take a closer look and maintain a steadfast application in our day to day lives. Let's not forget the words of 2 Timothy 3:16, "All scripture is God-breathed and is useful for teaching, rebuking, correcting and training in righteousness." The Bible is a tool meant for our edification and application.

Let's observe a few aspects on how we can adequately incorporate the Word into our everyday lives:

- Embrace Scripture in Personal Struggles - The faith heroes in the Bible faced immense challenges, be it Abraham's test of sacrifice, Paul's imprisonment, or David's struggle with sin. Their stories highlight how faith doesn't make us immune to problems but equips us for them. Personalizing Scripture in our struggles will provide daily guidance, comfort, and a renewed mind.
- Manifold Wisdom in Decision Making - Wisdom is a practical arm of faith, vital in navigating the maze of our decision-making process.

Proverbs is a potent book full of practical wisdom that provides guidance for interpersonal relationships, business dealings, financial stewardship, and moral integrity.

❖ Walking Love's Path – The stories in the Bible present a God of love, and one of the ways to be more godly is to be more loving. 1 Corinthians chapter 13 beautifully outlines the essence of love. Practicing such love in our daily lives enhances our spiritual strength and wellness.

❖ Prayer and Meditation - Philippians 4:6, "Do not be anxious about anything, but in every situation, by prayer and petition, with thanksgiving, present your requests to God." Prayer connects us to God, and His word inspires prayer. Meditation on scriptures gives a profound understanding and a fresh perspective on life.

The Word of God is indeed a living testament of transcendent truths and timeless wisdom. Merely reading it isn't enough; it demands a proactive approach. James 1:22 exhorts us, "Do not merely listen to the word, and so deceive yourselves. Do what it says." Let these biblical narratives be your guiding compass through life's tempestuous waves and uncertain winds. In doing so, you will feel the calming echoes of hope reverberate in your life, sustaining your faith's resilience for a serene and spiritually strong existence in today's world.

Journal Exercise:

Sit quietly for a moment and let your mind wander back through the chapter. Reflect upon your personal process of navigating the study and Bible readings.

1. Write down the strategies and approach that you have implemented while journeying through this study.
2. Enumerate three important principles or lessons you've learned from this chapter about navigating Bible study.
3. Give an example of a particular Bible story or verse you revisited or saw in new light due to this chapter's guidance. Explain why.
4. Finally, envision applying these Bible study strategies to everyday life scenarios. Describe one such scenario.

Remember, these reflections, just like your journey of faith, are deeply personal and there are no wrong responses. Your reflections help further illuminate your spiritual path and reinforce the lessons learned.

2
Genesis of Faith

2.1 The Foundation of Belief: Adam and Eve

In the cool confines of the Garden of Eden, God's first human creations, Adam and Eve, experienced an existence we can barely fathom: one free from sin. Their story, enshrined in the opening chapters of Genesis, finds its core not in their creation but in their fall from grace, a moment that altered the trajectory of every human life that followed. Yet within this stunning account of paradise lost, we find the germination of faith's resilience, an essential quality that has sustained people through the toughest trials of life, from personal strife to global upheaval. To peruse this story of primordial sin through a lens of hope and strength, we need to first delve into the implications of Adam and Eve's actions, both as individuals and as archetypes of humanity.

An apple, a crafty serpent, and an instance of disobedience; these are often what we associate with Adam and Eve's fall. The disobedience that led them to eating the forbidden fruit was not simply a blatant act of defiance against God but rather, it stemmed from a deeper issue: their lack of faith. This lack of faith, evidenced by their doubting God's intentions and character, led to them falling for the serpent's crafty deception. The fall was facilitated by their misguided desire to gain knowledge and become like God. Sin, as we see in this narrative, is multidimensional. It is rooted in disbelief, an inflated sense of self-worth and disobedience. All these factors work in concert, often subtly, to draw us away from our Creator. Moreover, this story reveals that sin's consequences are far from trivial; they're catastrophic and universal. Adam and Eve's disobedience resulted in their immediate expulsion from Eden, their loss of life-giving fellowship with God. The purity of their existence was disrupted, the ease of paradise replaced with toil and pain. Henceforth, humanity inherited this broken state, estranged from God, prone to sin, and trapped in a world permeated by suffering.

However, it doesn't end there. This narrative is also a story of faith's inception and resilience. At the moment of their downfall, God steps in. His immediate actions following the fall reveal His character: He is not only just, addressing the sin and assigning consequence, but He is also merciful and loving, making provisions for their survival outside Eden. By clothing them in animal skins, God tacitly affirmed His ongoing care for them - a powerful gesture of love that presented a ray of hope amid the terrifying new reality of their lives. This gesture also subtly echoed a profound truth: any shortcoming could be covered and any broken relationship could be mended by God's grace. It is here within these actions, we perceive God planting the seeds of faith and resilience in humanity, and giving us hope even in flawed reality.

This account of Adam and Eve, while narrating the origins of sin, also underlines the concept of redemption and resilience. A resilience that emerges only through acknowledging our imperfections, seeking God's grace, and endeavoring to orient our lives towards God's will, just like Adam and Eve had to do post their expulsion from Eden. Their struggle becomes our struggle, and it's through their narrative that we find glimpses of our own journey of faith. In the midst of chaos and uncertainty, we are called to lean into the hope and resilience that God so clearly demonstrated even in the face of humanity's first, most devastating fall from perfection.

The narrative of Eden's garden is not merely a tale of temptation and subsequent punishment, it is an insightful commentary on human nature and faith's resilience. Navigating through this portion of Biblical text affords us the opportunity to experience profound insights on faith's capacity to persist and deepen, even amidst moral tests. At its core, this narrative is about choice and accountability. Adam and Eve are given the freedom to eat from any tree within Eden's garden, with an enforced exception; the forbidden fruit with the knowledge of good and evil. The story's climax is reached when they yield to the serpent's temptation, breaking their covenant with God, and eating the fruit. They exerted their free will, opting for their immediate desires over their commitment. Yet, we glean more than just the consequences of breaking a divine command; we glimpse the resilient undercurrent of faith that grows from trials.

- ❖ Adam and Eve's actions didn't eradicate faith instead sprouted a resilient faith from their disobedience. As they were expelled from Eden's sanctuary, they faced the rough terrains of the world. Their faith did not waver in these tougher circumstances. On the contrary, it seemed to inculcate fresh perspectives into them, aiding them in navigating through the world.

- ❖ The grappling struggle with guilt and remorse further solidified their faith in the Divine. Countless times we witness individuals retreating to faith in their vulnerable moments. In this particular instance, they found solace and peace in their faith amidst the tumultuous aftershock of their decisions.
- ❖ God's enduring benevolence also became apparent. Even after their disobedience, when fashioning garments of skin, God provided for Adam and Eve. This act of unfathomable love could have very well rooted a resilient faith in them, testifying to the Divine's enduring mercy, despite their shortcoming.
- ❖ Redemption becomes a focal point of their faith journey post-Eden. The narrative emphasized hope and resilience, demonstrating that even when humans falter, they are tirelessly pursued by the Divine for restoration. The story hence transforms from a tale of disobedience to promise and hope, thereby addressing the modern human search for meaning beyond failure.
- ❖ Faith's resilience also imbued the concept of personal responsibility. Transgressing against God's command had its own repercussions. They made a choice, and faced consequences. This awareness prompted a greater sense of personal and spiritual responsibility, which can bolster and deepen one's faith.

As we reflect on these facets, we find a riveting exploration of faith's resilience amidst temptation and trials. The moral insights gleaned from Eden are timeless in their relevance and profound in their messages. By allowing these lessons to permeate our lives, we can solidify our faith and continually motivate ourselves towards spiritual maturation and resilience.

Event Number	Event Description	Event Significance
1	Creation of Adam	First human being in belief
2	Creation of Eve	First woman in belief
3	Garden of Eden	First dwelling place in belief
4	Serpent tempts Eve	First instance of temptation and disobedience
5	Eve tempts Adam	Start of shared culpability

Event Number	Event Description	Event Significance
6	Expulsion from Garden	Consequence and beginning of human struggle

Securing a stronghold on our spirituality and the marrow of our faith is chiseled by the lessons we draw from the initial sinners. The third chapter, Genesis, in the Bible, recounts the story of mankind's early ancestors, Adam and Eve, and their disobedience to God. They were the archetypes who ushered in a new epoch for humanity - one that was marked by struggle, conflict, and a constant yearning for salvation.

1. The reach of their sin was multifold, and this was the original incident that solidified the concept of 'actions have consequences.' When Adam and Eve disobeyed God and ate from the Tree of Knowledge, their disobedience cloaked all of humanity in sin. This sin was not merely about eating a forbidden fruit, but rather it was an insubordination against a divine decree. Their choice to listen to the serpent over God planted the seeds of distrust and rebellion.
2. With their disobedience, they lost their innocence. It alludes to the reality of human nature, wherein we develop an understanding of morality, conscience, and differentiating between right and wrong. They were expelled from Eden, stripped of their unique communion with God. They fell, and with their downfall, humanity was severed from its perfect unity with God.
3. However, the echo of hope resounds even in this seemingly dire narrative. For it offers a blueprint for redemption. The path back to spiritual unity and serenity is through confession, repentance, and striving to lead a virtuous life. Just as their action had profound implications, our actions today can also have enormous impacts. As we decipher the story of Adam and Eve, we should be motivated to lead actions that echo positivity, love, hope, and resilience.

Every story, including that of Adam and Eve, within the Bible, keenly illustrates a universal truth – our actions and choices leave an impact that reverberates through our lives and those around us – a ripple effect, if you may. The narrative of the first sinners, therefore, is not merely a tale of downfall, but rather a call to courageous living, acknowledgment of our flaws, when we falter, seeking forgiveness, and pledging to live better each day.

This quest for a righteous life, in sync with our divine purpose, is indeed spiritual strength in its purest form. It is where we find the resilience of faith - the capacity to keep reaching for the light despite stumbling down the darkest alleys. It is in the alignment of our actions with divine guidance that we discover serenity within this complex, modern world. By understanding and applying these profound teachings from our first ancestors' trials and transgressions, we throw a pebble of wisdom into the ocean of our life. The resulting ripples? A life empowered and enriched by spiritual strength, resilience, and serenity, echoing hope into every sphere of our existence. As we journey this path, we realize that these echoes are not just subtle resonances from ancient biblical times, they are powerful vibrations steering us towards a deeper understanding of our faith and strengthening our spiritual resilience.

So, remember, just as the first sinners, we are not immune to failure, but neither are we bereft of salvation. Raise a questioning mind, learn from the past, apply it in the present - and watch how beautifully and powerfully the echoes of hope resound in your life. Every tale in the bible, spoken or unspoken, is a lesson waiting to be embraced, so open that door, delve deep, and unearthed your spiritual strength and serenity.

Journal Exercise:

Recall the story of Adam and Eve as portrayed in chapter 2.1. Reflect deeply on their experience and decision-making process.

1. Write down your understanding of the concept of belief as it relates to the story of Adam and Eve. How might their experience reflect the development of your own beliefs?
2. Similarly to Adam and Eve, we often face conflicting facts or advice. When have you faced a situation where you had to question or confirm your beliefs? How did your beliefs guide your actions?
3. The story concludes with Adam and Eve receiving consequences for their actions. What do you think the story teaches us about taking responsibility for our belief-based action?
4. "The Foundation of Belief" is a significant phrase in the context of our faith journey. Can you identify and record the fundamental

beliefs that guide you in your life? How do these beliefs shape your world view?

Take 15 minutes to write down your reflections. You're encouraged not to judge what you write but simply to let your thoughts flow and see where your reflections lead.

2.2 The Legacy of Abraham: Faith Against All Odds

It would be an oversight not to mention the significant role Abraham, our common patriarch, has played in shaping our knowledge and understanding of faith's resilience. Archaeologists, historians, and theologians alike continue to uncover the layers of his character, largely defined by his profound willingness to obey the seemingly insurmountable callings of God. When we carefully dissect the life of Abraham, we encounter a man destined to become "a great nation" (Genesis 12:2), where his journey begins with unspeakable promises from an unproven God. Abraham's story is an expedition of obedience, even when God's commands seemed perplexing and contradictory to human understanding. From leaving his homeland to the binding of his son Isaac, Abraham made decisions that severely tested his faith, challenging every instinct, attachment, and reasoning he possessed. The call to leave his homeland and kin is the first significant litmus test of Abraham's faith. In Genesis 12:1-4, God asked Abraham to leave his country, his people, and his father's household and go to a land that God would show him. It was a daunting proposition indeed – to leave the familiar for an uncertain future in a place unknown. Yet, without hesitation, "Abram left, as the Lord had told him," and journeyed into the wilderness of faith's resilience. The decision to abandon everything familiar and embark on a journey into the unknown required vast resolve and an unwavering conviction in God's promises.

Another remarkable moment in Abraham's journey is God's bewildering command in Genesis 22 to sacrifice Abraham's only son, the son of his love, Isaac. The very son God previously affirmed would continue Abraham's lineage was now commanded to be a burnt offering on a mountain. This event, often coined as the Akedah or the Binding of Isaac, is a cornerstone narrative in all three monotheistic religions' traditions. Yet, once again, confronted with an unthinkable request, Abraham displayed an unwavering commitment to God's directives. Despite analysts' ongoing debates surrounding the ethical ramifications of such an episode, the overarching narrative places Abraham as an analogous sign of unparalleled resilience to an enduring faith. Even as he ascended the mountain and bound his son for sacrifice, his convictions remained steadfast, an echo of hope that resonated within his heart. He held onto the assurance of God's words despite the incongruities of his current circumstances.

Abraham's story isn't just about making hard decisions; it's about unwavering convictions – a testament to the strength of an enduring faith. His life's narrative invites us to reflect on our own. Are we willing to lean into the unknown with God? Can we embrace uncomfortable and seemingly irrational directives, trusting in His ultimate plan? We learn that sometimes the unlikely path is the one on which we find our greatest spiritual growth and understanding. Abraham's life reassures us that our faith's resilience isn't about having all the answers – it's about trusting in the one who does.

Continuing our exploration within the narrative, we now direct our attention toward the vital covenant between God and Abraham. The tendrils of this covenant spread out and became the foundation of so many stories and prophecies that we see later in scripture, but also continue to be a source of strength and enlightenment for each one of us as modern spiritual seekers. The relationship between Abraham and God serves as a valuable framework in deciphering the often elusive discourse surrounding faith and promises in religion. The symbolism and intricacies enclosed in the blessings offered to Abraham and his descendants transcend the confines of their historical context, finding resonance in our contemporary lives and struggles.

In the very core of their exchange lies a promise from God — a commitment of abundant blessings and prosperity to Abraham and his descendants. This vow manifests in numerous ways throughout Abraham's journey, but it is in Genesis 13:16 in which God declares to Abraham, "I will make your offspring like the dust of the earth, so that if anyone could count the dust, then your offspring could be counted." The immensity of this promise, rendering Abraham's descendants as numerous as the earth's dust, unbounded and innumerable, cannot be overstated. Yet, this emblematic expression was not merely about growth in numbers. It was a testament to resilience, an underlying motif of endurance and faith in the face of adversity.

In our own lives, we can extract several profound insights from this covenant.

- ❖ It Places Faith at the Center: Abraham was no extraordinary being. He was an average man asked to believe in a vast promise. His faith, strong and unwavering, holds an important lesson- faith can be our strongest asset in times of doubt.

- ❖ It Emphasizes Promises Outlast Challenges: Abraham was subjected to several trials and tribulations before the promise came to fruition. We often find ourselves stuck in tough spots; it's significant to understand it's not a dead end but a testing period for our faith and determination.
- ❖ It Reminds us of the Certainty of God's Promises: The covenant underscores God's unwavering commitment towards His promises.
- ❖ It Upholds the Concept of Blessings: This covenant teaches us that blessings often come with an obligation. They are not merely something received but something to be lived up to, ensuring we remain dedicated to our spiritual responsibilities.

Examining this covenant affords us a perspective — a way of understanding life's challenges and promises in a deeper, more faith-driven way. It imparts an understanding that our journey will be fraught with difficulties, but a consistent belief in divine resilience can guide us through, with our faith becoming stronger, just like Abraham's. This resilience is what affords us the ability to turn challenges into spiritual growth opportunities, fulfilling our own covenants with our faith and spiritual path.

Year	Event	Significance
1800 BC	Birth of Abraham	Start of Abraham's faith journey
1780 BC	God's Covenant with Abraham	Establishment of the Israelite lineage
1755 BC	Sacrifice of Isaac	Test of Abraham's faith
1750 BC	Death of Sarah	End of Abraham's lifelong companion
1730 BC	Death of Abraham	End of Abraham's life and legacy

Abraham's tests were unparalleled in their intensity and complexity, painting an exquisite picture of faith's resilience in the face of adversity. These trials were of various forms—lose his homeland, be childless into old age, endanger his wife, and even sacrifice his son—enough to smother flickering spirits of faith. Yet the patriarch emerged, neither broken nor beclouded. His stories stir within us a realization that our furnaces of affliction can also shape us, not stifle us.

Delving deeper into Abraham's life, consider his journey out of his homeland, an event that threw him into a cauldron of uncertainty. His dearest ties were to be severed without clear details of his future home or his fated health, family and fortune. But rather than resist, he responded with obedience and trust in divine providence. We, too, often find ourselves jettisoned into unfamiliar territories. At our disposal then is the lesson from Abraham—trust the process and surrender to God's greater wisdom. Furthermore, the promise of an heir was also a painstaking test for Abraham, made more stringent with the slow tick of passing decades. Every crease in his face and silver hair was a memento of delay. Nonetheless, Abraham remained steadfast, hoping against all hope, and eventually witnessed the miracle of Isaac. His unwavering faith is a beacon for us when God's promises seem distant and unanswered prayers pile up. It firmly propounds, hold on to faith, even when there's little left to hold it with.

Abraham's willingness to sacrifice Isaac is perhaps the zenith of his spiritual strength, and a pinnacle in the Bible's exposition of faith. Imagine the torment of a father asked to kill his long-awaited child! Yet Abraham did not hesitate, did not argue, but prepared to obey. God intervened at the last minute, sparing Isaac, proving the trial was not about death, but about faith. This story is pertinent today when our convictions are flung into the pit. Abraham's example encourages us to always put God first, even when the cost is dear and unfathomable. Finally, when Sarah was endangered, superficially, it seems Abraham faltered by lying about their relationship. However, a closer look reveals his intent was to protect her, banking again on his faith in God's protection. When our loved ones are at risk, following Abraham's model means making choices that can incite criticism but emanate from confidence in divine grace.

From Abraham's trials, we glean vital lessons that catapult our spiritual resilience. Firstly, trusting in God's plans, even when they seem nebulous and daunting. Secondly, never twine your faith with conditions or timelines; God isn't late; He's strategic. Thirdly, love God above all, even when it pierces like a sacrificial knife. Finally, stand fearless when your faith choices seem confusing or contentious to the world. As we survive our furnaces of affliction, armed with these lessons, our situations won't necessarily change, but we will—we become sturdier, shinier, and more sanctified versions of who we were. We perceive God's sovereignty in spite of our affliction and experience an echo of hope amid the tumult of trials, just like Abraham. This fills us with an immutable serenity and imparts a spiritual strength that, unlike regular might, thrives on adversities, not despite them. Abraham's story then isn't past but is perpetually current, ceaselessly uncloaking dimensions of faith to support our spiritual survival in this modern world.

Journal Exercise:

1. Describe a situation in your life where you felt like Abraham, asked to believe in something against all odds. What was the situation and how did you respond to it?
2. Reflect on the promises God made to Abraham. In what ways do you see God's promises manifesting in your life?
3. Abraham's faith didn't waver even when things did not seem to go as God had promised. Assess a circumstance where your faith wavered due to unexpected detours. What would your reaction have been if you handled it with unwavering faith like Abraham?
4. Remember moments of doubt. Write about how you could utilize Abraham's example to navigate through uncertainty in the future.
5. Illustrate the long wait of Abraham and Sarah for their promised child, Isaac. Write about a long wait you are enduring in your life. How does this relate to your spiritual strength and trust in God's timing?
6. Drawing from Abraham's example, write a personal pledge of faith and resilience, to remind yourself of God's promises during tough times.

2.3 Lessons from Joseph: Resilience in Adversity

Jacob, the father of all Israelites, blessed his most adored son, Joseph, with a flamboyant coat whose colors surpassed the spectrum of the rainbow. This prized gift stirred an intense storm of envy and betrayal within Joseph's own blood - his brothers.

Joseph was more than a proud owner of a beautiful coat; he was a man of visions. His dreams, which he innocently recounted to his brothers, sparked both resentment and rage. He saw himself as a sheaf standing tall above the rest while other sheaves bow before him. In yet another dream, he saw himself as a prominent star, the sun and moon, and eleven stars were bowing down to him. Unaware of the toxic jealousy festering in his brothers' hearts, Joseph opened the door wide to betrayal. Yet, these unfolding events were shaping a foundation of resilience that would stand unshaken during the most formidable storms and trials. The narrative introduced us to a young man plunged into pits, disowned by his own siblings, and sold like a commodity to a land of strangers. However, it pushed him onto the stage of a life-changing episode where he emerged even stronger, resilient, and more focused. Joseph's journey from the pits to the pinnacle powerfully echoes the essence of resilience in faith and beckons us to not merely observe, but interact with the story. It invites us to step into Joseph's sandals and walk the rocky road leading to serenity and spiritual strength that emanated from his unwavering reliance on God.

The colorful coat was a symbol of favor, but it also pointed towards distinct individual qualities which set him apart:

- Dreamer: Despite being perceived as high-headed and arrogant for sharing his dreams, Joseph was a dreamer. His grand dreams of spheres bowing before him spoke volumes about his belief in the beauty and good of his future. This storytelling, imbued with faith, encouraged resilience as he faced harsh trials and tribulations.
- Resilient Faith: Despite being abandoned by his brothers, his faith did not wane, but rather grew. His resilience was born out of enduring faith and trust, as he believed in the faithfulness of God.
- Intense Wellspring of Forgiveness: When a day of reconciliation came, he embraced his brothers rather than condemning them, demonstrating that spiritual strength can eclipse the power of bitterness and revenge. His forgiveness was a testament to his extraordinary spiritual strength, borne out of his faith in God's ultimate plan.

The episodes of Joseph's life remind us that being favored or blessed does not shield us from trials. Challenges are a part of our journeys that shape us and cultivate within us the seeds for resilience. Faith's resilience goes beyond the surface; it travels to the heart of belief, trust, and reliance on the divine, showing us that even in the midst of dire straits, there is a surreal serenity that comes from unwavering trust in God's promises.

Lesson Number	Key Takeaway	Impact on Life
1	Embracing Challenges	Increased mental strength
2	Forgiveness over Grudges	Improved relationships
3	Trusting God in Hard Times	Deepen faith and patience
4	Persistence in the face of Adversity	Boost determination
5	Positive Outlook during Difficulties	Enhanced mental wellbeing
6	Transformation through Trials	Character development

As we delve into the life of Joseph, we find a man whose faith echoed through the harrowing trials he faced. Abandoned by his own siblings into the deep well of their jealousy, sold into slavery, falsely accused by his master's wife, and thrown into prison, Joseph could have easily succumbed to despair.

But contrary to what one might expect, Joseph prevailed. He went on to become the Prime Minister in Egypt, ultimately preventing a famine that could have claimed numerous lives, including those of his own brothers. His faith, resilience, and patience were proven through his trials, becoming an echo of hope across the annals of scripture. How did he remain steadfast in the face of an undulating journey from the favor of his father to the pit of despair and finally to the palace of redemption? The answer lies in his utter reliance on his divine connection. Despite the trials he faced, Joseph understood that they were not random events but part of a divine plan, a tapestry that the Divine Weaver was skillfully creating.

From our limited perspective, life often appears as a chaotic jumble of threads. However, Joseph had the insight to perceive God's handiwork even amid chaos, much like a weaver who maintains a steady hand in the process of creating a intricate pattern.

- In the prison, pit, and the palace, Joseph turned to God. Regardless of the change in his circumstances, his faith remained unwavering. In the face of injustice, imprisonment, and tribulation, his primary concern was about breaking God's decrees. He portrayed what the Apostle Paul would later preach in Romans 8:28 that "God causes all things to work together for good."

- ❖ He remained hopeful and understood that God's silence is not His absence. Despite his cries for help to the butler and the baker being initially unheeded, he remained confident in his deliverance by the Lord. This reflects Psalm 27:14: "Wait for the Lord; be strong, and let your heart take courage; wait for the Lord!"
- ❖ Repeatedly, Joseph showed that faith in the Divine should supersede fear of human enemies. He understood God's power and mercy beyond the materialistic limitations and human comprehension. His ability to forgive his brothers for their actions is a testament to this understanding.

Ultimately, if you look closely at Joseph's life, you would realize that the narrative communicates a powerful and symbolic representation of faith. It is not about escaping trials but weathering them with hope and endurance, using them as a stepping stone on the road to spiritual growth and serenity. His story reveals that the undulations of life can either make one bitter or better, and faith determines which course one takes.

Echoes of hope sound the loudest in the valleys of despair. As you navigate the tumultuous terrains of your life, may Joseph's life serve as an echo of hope, resilience, and divine assurance, reminding you that the same God who saw him through is still on the throne, weaving together the various threads of our lives into a beautiful tapestry. Despite the challenges of the years of famine, Joseph's faith held strong, and the grain storehouses he had built stood tall, brimming with the nation's vital sustenance. Recall how he led with tenacity and resilience, turning a predicted disaster into a period of growth and survival. In these years, not only did Egypt prosper, but so did its people, through the benefaction of these storehouses established by their wise and faithful leader.

Reflect upon how these overflowing granaries are symbolic of Joseph's faith - resilient, bountiful, and life-giving. Amid trials, Joseph's faith not only sustained him but also supplied sustenance to a whole nation on the brink of demise. His unwavering belief in a providential plan endured, fortifying those around him, instilling hope, and enabling survival.

Consider these key understandings from this chapter in Joseph's life:

* True faith can turn circumstances of scarcity into abundance. Though the land was barren, the storehouses of Egypt, meticulously filled under Joseph's command, were a testament to the ability of faith to provide an oasis of sustenance amidst drought.

* Faith manifests in actions, not just words. Joseph's wisdom and initiative were the physical expressions of his abiding faith. Building storehouses was a practical, tangible demonstration of his deep-rooted belief in God's prophetic voice.

* Faithful resilience brings prosperity. Joseph's faith broke the vicious cycle of fear, uncertainty, and potential tragedy and created a virtuous cycle of hope, relief, and growth.

Even amidst such prosperity, remember Joseph's story continued with an even more profound lesson about faith – the lesson of forgiveness. Encountering his brothers years after their unforgivable act of betrayal brought Joseph's faith strength to the forefront again.

His brothers, seeking aid in the land of Egypt, were unaware that the generous and powerful man before whom they knelt was the same person they had maliciously disposed of years ago. Joseph was now in a position of power having the ability to punish or even execute his brothers, yet he chose an alternate path. Unfathomable to most of us, this act holds unimaginable strength, born of faith and grace. Joseph, through his spiritual resilience, saw beyond his personal pain and offered his brothers forgiveness, choosing love over revenge, unity over estrangement, and peace over conflict.

Reflect on these key understandings from Joseph's profound act of forgiveness:

* Faith brings strength to forgive. Despite the possible desire for revenge, Joseph's resilient faith empowered him to rise above his personal hurt and forgive his brothers, an act that bound his family back together in love.

* Faith lifts us above our circumstances. Having the power to exact retribution yet choosing differently demonstrates that Joseph's spiritually rich approach permitted him to see life from a higher perspective.

* Faith fosters serenity. Joseph's decision to forgive his bothers demonstrates how faith can lead us to a place of tranquility, shattering the chains of resentment and anger.

Faith is not only our shield in trying times but also our guiding compass towards serenity, wisdom, prosperity, and forgiveness. As we traverse our own life's journey, let's strive to integrate such resilient faith into our own spiritual practice, one that actively reflects in our actions and attitudes, bearing fruits of endurance, understanding, and compassion.

Journal Exercise:

Begin by writing a brief summary of Joseph's journey and how he demonstrated resilience during his adversities. Reflect on a time in your life where you've experienced hardships and note the strategies you used to weather through these challenges. Now, compare your own experience with that of Joseph's. What lessons can you draw from his realistic yet optimistic attitude? How can you apply these lessons to strengthen your own faith and resilience?

Next, create a list of three to five personal affirmation statements inspired by Joseph's resilience. These should focus on your ability to triumph in the face of adversity, relying on your faith for strength. Revisit and repeat these affirmations daily for a week and observe any changes in your mindset or spirit.

Lastly, jot down a prayer seeking guidance, strength, and resilience in the face of present or future adversity, inspired by Joseph's story. Reflect upon this prayer whenever you feel disheartened or defeated.

How did this exercise impact your feelings and perceptions towards hardships? Do you see challenges differently? Observe and record your feelings and thoughts on this transformation.

2.4 The Complexity of Jacob: Wrestling with God and Man

Diving deeply into the annals of biblical accounts, the story of Jacob presents a picture of human frailty and also the power of persistence in seeking divine favor. In this intricate narrative, we encounter a man that is as famous for his weaknesses as he is for his strength. On a fateful day, Jacob, wrestling with both internal and external elements of his existence, made what appears to be an inconsequential exchange with his elder brother, Esau. However, what transpired in that moment was far from trivial. It was a birthright bargain; a pivotal point that would forever change the dynamic of their relationship and the course of their lives. Jacob, like every human, was enveloped in the reality of human weakness. It's paramount to reflect on the fact that he was driven more by necessity and less by an unquenchable thirst for power or wealth when he requested Esau's birthright. In context, his actions were direct responses to the circumstances surrounding him. This is not to justify his actions but to empathize with his human condition.

Ponder for a moment on Jacob's circumstance: He set forth to leverage Esau's momentary vulnerability and carnal cravings for instant gratification, and used it to secure a future that seemed uncertain to him. Jacob was desperate, seeking a validation that appeared elusive due to his position as the second-born. This led him to seize an opportunity, bold and delicate as it might seem. Here we see that the dynamics of divine favor transcend human error and impatience. It weaves through our human actions, decisions, faults, and strengths, encoding divine wisdom upon the canvass of humanity. Divine grace doesn't connive with human weakness, but it also doesn't abandon us in our vulnerable moments, our times of desperation or uninformed decisions. Rather, grace extends an unrelenting hand of redemption, a never-failing beacon of hope. Added to this, Jacob was entwined in the culture of his time where customs and traditions placed greater privileges and responsibilities on the firstborn. This cultural practice posed an existential dilemma to Jacob. It subtly suggested that his fate may forever be locked in the shadow of his elder brother. But Jacob's story illuminates a pathway for us- a pathway that dances in the echoes of hope, affirming that divine favor is a reality that we can embrace, despite our frailty or the biased cultural or societal structures that may surround us.

Keep in mind, however, that our actions have consequences. For Jacob, his decision, borne out of desperation, led to years of struggle, pain and separation from his family. However, it was these very struggles that shaped him, refined him, and ultimately molded him into a man that was ready to fulfill divine destiny upon his life. He wrestled with beings both divine and human, persisting until he received his blessing. Thus, Jacob's story reminds us that our failures, desperation, or missteps can never disqualify us from the experience of divine favor. What matters is our resilience and unfailing hope, the willingness to wrestle, to persist, and to strip ourselves of guile and deception as Jacob did. Only then, we can start hearing the whispers of hope faintly echoing in the corners of our reality. It is at this juncture that we start experiencing the reality of divine favor and reach for our full potential.

Transitioning fluidly from our previous delve into Jacob's life, we reach the pivotal moment of Jacob's dream of a ladder. An unbroken line of communication between heaven and earth, potent with symbolic resonance. In this narrative, Jacob dreams of a ladder, or the stairways to heaven, with angels moving up and down the rungs. God stands at the top of the ladder, offering a renewed covenant to Jacob. This encounter, suffused with the divine, affirms the dynamic presence of God not only in our lives but also in our dreams. This marks a turning point in Jacob's life – radicalizing his faith, redirecting his purpose. Exploring the symbolic resonance of the staircase can yield profound insights about our spiritual ascendancy. The ladder signifies that we are not alone in our battles; we are embedded within a grand cosmic journey.

- The Rungs: Life is replete with adversities, brimming with trials and tribulations. Each rung of the ladder symbolizes these episodic challenges that man must surmount in his quest for God.
- The Ladder: The ladder is a compelling symbol of progress, of constant upwards propulsion. It underscores the belief that, despite the adversities that life presents us, we are capable of transcending them.
- The Angels: The angels ascending and descending the ladder are reminders of God's omnipresence and collaborative role in our spiritual progress. They embody messages of divine love, reassurance, and guidance, perched on the ladder of life.

Jacob's spiritual eye was opened in the solitude of the night, laying bare the reality of God's omnipresence. This dream is a lesson in the transformational power of faith when connections to the Divine are deeply nurtured. Dreams tend to be discounted as chaff, but our subconscious can often serve as a conduit to divine revelation. Jacob's dream bespeaks the spiritual power of dreams as a pathway to revelation and transformation. This narrative imparts that through faith, we are given eyes to see the unseen; the mundane reality transcends into visionary manifestations of the divine. When we have faith, our lives are no longer confined by temporal limitations; instead, they become powerfully interwoven into the divine universal narrative. The divine revelation in the dream confirms the faith and promise God had for Jacob, despite his delinquency. How can we contextually apply Jacob's encounter to our daily life? It's a moving testament to God's unending mercies. For every stumble, misstep, or fall in our lives, His angels are there, guiding and propelling us further up the staircase.

This narrative imparts, once again, an essential truth: faith is a transformative, sanctifying encounter that radically changes and emboldens us. It is not an escape from life's struggle, but an ascent informed by struggle. Like Jacob, let us harness adversity through the triumphant power of faith and use it as a stepping-stone to achieve spiritual ascendancy.

Themes	Key Ideas
Identity Crisis	Struggle for truth and wholeness
Divine Encounter	Realization of divine presence
Self Perception	Evolution from deceiver to chosen
Blessings and Curses	Revelation of celestial power
Human Relationships	Interactions with Esau and Laban
Life Transformations	Impacts of divine and mortal wrestling

Jacob's night of wrestling at Penuel offers a vivid illustration of faith's resilience and God's patient, loving engagement in the human struggle. As darkness fell, it was an anxious time for Jacob, who was about to face Esau, his twin brother he once tricked. In the midst of this inner turmoil, he was confronted by a mysterious figure who grappled with him until dawn. The physical struggle mirrored his lifelong emotional and spiritual battles - wrestling with his guilt, his fear, and ultimately his faith.

Several insights emerge from this encounter:

- It demonstrated God's willingness to engage with human struggles. God did not dismiss or belittle Jacob's fear. Instead, He stepped into the wrestling match, physically participating in Jacob's struggle.
- The wrestling match signified Jacob's stubborn resilience. Despite the struggle, he refused to back down. He had the will to persist, to stick with the fight despite his fear and even physical pain. This resilience would define him and forever mark his relationship with God.

- The iconic moment came when the stranger asked Jacob to release him. However, Jacob insisted on a blessing before letting him go. This intense desire for divine blessing underscores Jacob's faith, and it signified his determination to seek God's favor no matter the cost.
- From this struggle, Jacob emerged with a new identity, a personal triumph steeped in faith's resilience. Formerly known as the 'heel-catcher' or the 'deceiver,' he was given a new name: Israel, meaning 'he who strives with God.' This change wasn't superficial or honorary. It reflected his profound transformation through wrestling with God and emerging renewed, resilient, and imbued with spiritual strength.
- The struggle left Jacob with a pronounced limp, a reminder of his encounter with God. This seemed to underscore that learning, change, and spiritual growth often come with scars but these marks are not symbols of defeat rather, emblems of faith's resilience.

Jacob's story invites us to embrace our struggles, not shy away from them. It teaches us that God will meet us in our darkest hours, wrestling with us and imparting lessons that deepen our faith. His wrestling match wasn't just about survival. It signified the transformation of his inner self, a shift that brought him into a deeper relationship with God. Thus, modern-day believers might draw solace and strength from Jacob's experience. Life today often feels like a wrestling match – with worries, insecurities, crises, and unrelenting expectations. Jacob's story reminds us that these encounters, as difficult as they may be, can be avenues for discovering and experiencing God anew. It encourages us to lean into our struggles and persist in faith, knowing that in the wrestling, we can experience divine resilience and find serenity amidst the storm. But of course, this isn't a suggestion to seek out struggles or create unnecessary strife. Rather, it's about changing our perspective, to see trials as opportunities to deepen our faith, to wrestle and emerge resilient, blessed, and more attuned to God's presence in our lives, mirroring echoes of hope in our soul. As we do so, we'll likely find our spiritual muscles strengthening, toughened by the contest yet softened by divine love. And, like Jacob, we might even come away limping, but walking more closely with God.

Journal Exercise:

1. Identify two key moments within the story of Jacob wrestling with God and Man that struck you the most. Describe these moments in your own words, and explain why they had an impact on you.

2. Reflect on a time you have wrestled with your faith or life decisions in the same manner Jacob did. How did that impact your spiritual development and personal growth?
3. How does Jacob's encounter with God in the story influence your views on spiritual resilience? What aspects of Jacob's resilience do you see in yourself and where would you like to grow?
4. Write a prayer or affirmation inspired by Jacob's journey that you can use when you face struggles in your personal life.
5. Draw a parallel from Jacob's experiences to today's world. What lessons can be drawn from Jacob's complexity that applies to modern society?

Remember, the objective of your reflection is helping you decipher the meaning behind biblical stories and allow you to create deeper connections between your personal experiences and spiritual teachings.

3
Exodus: The Journey of Faith

3.1 Moses: From Prince to Prophet

Raised in luxury in the heart of Egypt, the man we now know as Moses experienced a transformational journey that echoes through time, inspiring millions with its tale of faith's resilience. With the Nile's currents as his playground and the royal court as his classroom, young Moses grew from a prince of Egypt to a prophet of God. Historical records, as well as findings in archaeology and anthropology, suggest that Moses' upbringing in Egypt was a significant influence on his outlook and his mission. This part of Moses' life was foundational in his spiritual growth, and it is crucial to understanding the potent lessons that his story brings us today.

In the city of Thebes, he had the invaluable opportunity to experience the full range of human social constructs, from kings and queens to slaves and masters. Rising under the teachings of Egyptian educators, Moses became familiar with the mystics of ancient Egyptian religion. Yet, it was not the path of a Pharaoh nor the mysticism that would define his destiny, but his heritage as an Israelite. The story of Moses provides us with a significant teaching: where we start in life does not determine where we can go. His life serves as a reminder of the universality of faith's resilience. No matter your circumstances, the ability to hold steadfast in your belief and weather the storms life throws at us is within your grasp.

Countless Bible stories remind us that often, it's in the moments of our greatest adversity that we find our greatest strength. Moses, a fearsome leader forged in the crucibles of royalty and slavery, epitomizes this principle. It is in his struggles that we see his courage shine, and it is in his unwavering faith that we witness his fortitude. Moses' metamorphosis from

Egyptian prince to Hebrew prophet provides an invaluable perspective for the modern seeker aspiring for spiritual strength. His journey invites us to:

- Embrace change and transformation: Moses' journey from an Egyptian prince to a Hebrew prophet was not a simple path. This change shaped him into a resilient figure with a higher purpose. Our lives are in constant flux, and sometimes it's the unexpected changes that lead us down the most rewarding paths.
- Foster open-mindedness: As a prince exposed to a myriad of beliefs and cultures, Moses developed a rich understanding of the world, which later played a crucial role in his leadership. Our diverse world offers endless opportunities to learn and grow. Be open and receptive to varying cultures, ideas, and beliefs.
- Cultivate empathy: Moses' experiences, both as a prince and a shepherd, taught him to empathize with different walks of life. Empathy can be a game-changer in our interactions with others, and in turn, our spiritual growth.

The biblical account of Moses discloses that he was born in adversity, raised in privilege, and called to rescue his people from bondage. His life path stands as a testament of resilience and a beacon of inspiration for anyone seeking spiritual strength amidst their personal struggles. His account from a royal palace in Egypt to the wilderness of Midian and finally leading his people to liberation depicts a truly transformational journey.

This chapter of biblical history whispers to us the echoes of hope that resonate in our quests for serenity, resilience, and spiritual strength. As we venture deeper into the life and mission of Moses, it is impossible not to acknowledge the significance of the burning bush, a divine manifestation and an introduction to God's master plan for the Israelites. Moses was shepherding his father-in-law's sheep when he came across a bush that was on fire but was not consumed. Interested and intrigued, he drew nearer. It was in this instance when God spoke directly to him. This extraordinary event was Moses' awakening to his mission, and it marked the starting point of his unparalleled spiritual journey. The voice emanating from the bush was the voice of Yahweh, the God of his ancestors-- Abraham, Isaac, and Jacob. Through this ethereal encounter, Moses received instructions to liberate the children of Israel from the clutches of Pharaoh and deliver them to a land flowing with milk and honey. Realizing the magnanimity and complexity of this task, Moses was initially hesitant. He questioned his capabilities and feared the unbelief of the people. It was here, God provided Moses with profound wisdom and signified his unwavering support.

A potent symbol of God's recurrent presence during the arduous journey Moses was about to undertake was his staff. When cast down, it turned into a serpent-- illustrating the divine power he was granted to convince the skeptics and confront the oppressors. This event reminds us that even in our times of self-doubt, apparent-assured tools or skills could be transformed into powerful resources by divine aid. Following his divine epiphany, Moses journeyed back to Egypt, armed with God's assurance and invigorated by a renewed faith. What ensued was a series of forewarnings, plagues, and miracles, which eventually led to the liberations of the Israelites from the Pharaoh's oppressive reign.

The exodus from Egypt wasn't the end but merely a transitory phase in this journey towards spiritual strength. It served as a physical liberation and a metaphorical emancipation from the mental shackles. Transitioning towards Sinai, the travelers with Moses gradually transitioned from being a group of distraught persons to a congregation of believers. As they set foot on Sinai's slopes, Moses ascended its peaks alone to commune with God. He stayed for forty days and forty nights, during which he received the Ten Commandments – the Divine's chosen code of conduct for humanity. The Commandments marked a pivotal point of spiritual and moral guidance. They laid down principles of worship, instructions for personal interactions, societal obligations, and absolute moral laws— the contemplation of which can ignite a sense of direction in our modern lives.

The journey of Moses from the burning bush to the peaks of Sinai is a testament to faith's resilience. It serves as a beacon of hope, reminding us that during our most challenging trials and periods of self-doubt, unwavering faith can lead to liberation and enlightenment. Delving deeper into this journey, we can discover countless lessons that apply to our lives today— mirror reflections of the struggles we face and continuous assurances of divine assistance on our path towards spiritual strength. An important dimension of spiritual strength and serenity lies in understanding the resilience of faith, even amid adversity. And, one can find no better proof than Moses, who leads his people out of Egypt and through the wilderness. The narrative of Moses is a testament to the enduring power of faith and an illustration of the journey that every spiritual individual undertakes at some point.

It could be said that Moses himself faced significant adversity as soon as he was born. Cast into the river inside a papyrus basket to escape Pharaoh's decree of death on all newborn Hebrew boys, it was nothing short of a miracle that Pharaoh's daughter found him and raised him in the palace. This early brush with adversity set the tone for Moses' life and his unique relationship with God.

Then comes The Exodus, the departure of the Israelites from Egypt. The enormity of the task placed on Moses' shoulders was tremendous; he had to lead hundreds of thousands of people to freedom, breaking the chains of their oppressors, and guiding them through the uncertainty of wilderness away from what had been home. It was a massive test of faith, and Moses took it on - his hope and faith leading the way. Throughout the journey, the Israelites grumbled, doubted, and even openly revolted, challenging Moses' leadership. And, despite the negativity, Moses remained resilient. He struggled, questioned, and sometimes, held God to account, but he never lost his faith. Amid adversity, his faith was resilient, anchoring him in the tempestuous storm of doubt, fear, and uncertainty. Then we have the experience of wanderings in the wilderness, which lasted forty years. Could anything be more adverse than being lost in a wilderness, not for days or months, but for years? Again, this story showcases Moses' unwavering faith, providing three crucial insights arising from this narrative of resilience:

- Patience and Perseverance: Moses' persistent faith despite the harsh conditions of the wilderness teaches us the power of patience and perseverance. It emphasizes the need to hold on even when conditions are unfavorable.
- God's Guidance: The story symbolizes God's guidance, signifying that even in the bleakest of circumstances, a higher power guides us.
- Hope for the Promised Land: Despite the grim reality of the wilderness, Moses kept the hope of the Promised Land alive, reminding us that the destination is worth the journey.

As we explore the spiritual strength of Moses, we encounter the profound truth that our faith, like that of Moses, can endure and overcome even the severest of adversities. We learn the importance of keeping our faith alive, even when circumstances appear insurmountable. We see the necessity of holding onto hope, even when it seems like there's nothing left to hope for. And through all this, we come to understand how our faith can likewise serve as a beacon of resilience, guiding us through the wilderness of our own adversities and leading us to our Promised Land: a place of spiritual serenity and strength.

Life Stage	Key Event	Significance
Prince of Egypt	Adopted by Pharaoh's Daughter	Raised in Royalty
Fugitive	Fleeing after Murder	Exile to Midian
Shepherd	Marriage to Zipporah	Settling into New Life
Prophet	Burning Bush Revelation	Divine Commissioning
Liberator	Plagues on Egypt	Deliverance of Israelites
Law Giver	Ten Commandments	Sacred Covenant

Journal Exercise:

Begin by summarizing your understanding of Moses' life transformation, from prince to prophet. In which ways do you resonate with his journey?

Next, write down any significant changes you have experienced in your own life. How has your faith contributed or influenced during those transformations?

Reflect on Moses' doubts and insecurities when he was called by God at the burning bush. Share a time you have felt unqualified or unequipped for a task or role; how did you respond and what was the outcome?

Finally, Moses relied heavily on his faith as he led the Israelites. In what aspects of your life do you feel the need for greater reliance on faith? What steps can you take this week to cultivate this faith?

3.2 The Red Sea: Miracles in Desperation

The Red Sea Miracle is an integral story in the Bible that bears testament to the resilience of faith amidst seemingly insurmountable obstacles. Trapped between an oppressive enemy force and what looked like a fatal dead-end, the Israelites were cornered. The circumstances that led to this event are filled with dread, helplessness and utter desperation. Not so long before this moment, the Israelites, under the guidance of Moses, had gained their freedom from the brutal regime of the Pharaoh of Egypt, a massive turning point that promised a future free from the chains of bondage. This newfound freedom, however, was rapidly threatened when the Pharaoh, filled with spite and regret, led his army in pursuit of the Israelites to bring them back into the captivity they had just escaped from.

The Israelites were on the brink of seeing their dreams of liberation crumble. The approaching Egyptian force on one hand and the unyielding Red Sea on the other cast a shadow of despair over them. They were in a place where their envisioned future seemed impossible; their faith was on the edge, their hope wafer-thin. Instead of seeing liberation and triumph on the horizon, they saw a horrifying spectacle of a raging enemy closing in. Their hearts filled with fear, they questioned Moses in despair "Is it because there are no graves in Egypt that you have taken us away to die in the wilderness?" (Exodus 14:11). This moment was a true test of faith. They were at a crossroads where they could either succumb to their fears or hold steadfast to their faith in God's promise of liberation. The desperation preceding the Red Sea Miracle is palpable. It ushers us into an intimate understanding of the fears that haunted the hearts of the Israelites, displaying how much courage it took to remain faithful when everything seemed to be falling apart, and how extraordinary their faith was amidst such extreme obstacles.

It was in this bleak place surrounded by despair, that the resilience of faith transformed both the physical and spiritual reality of the Israelites. As Moses lifted his staff over the Red Sea, an east wind blew strongly all night, parting the waters and etching a path of freedom for the Israelites. This was God's miraculous intervention, demonstrating His unfailing promise to deliver those who put their trust in Him. The Red Sea Miracle reveals a divine truth - faith can thrive amid obstacles. No matter how dire the situation may appear, faith sees beyond the visible circumstances. It builds on hope, anchored in God's promises. The desperation preceding the miracle wasn't merely an obstacle; it was a prerequisite for the manifestation of God's power. It reminds us that faith's resilience amid obstacles is not built on the absence of desperation but on perseverance and trust in God's promises, even in the darkest of times.

Event	Description	Time Period
Crossing of the Red Sea	Moses led the Israelites	Around 1446 BC

Event	Description	Time Period
Waters Parted	A Miracle performed by Moses	Brief Moment in 1446 BC
Drowning of Pharaoh's Army	Egyptian forces were drowned	Shortly after Crossing in 1446 BC
Desert Journey	Began after crossing the Red Sea	1446-1406 BC
Manna and Quail	God provided food in wilderness	Daily during Desert Journey
Water from Rock	Another miracle in the desert	Occurred during Desert Journey

Starting from the comfort of their homes in Egypt, pursued by the strongest army in the known world, the Israelites found themselves hemmed in by the Red Sea. With no human resolution in sight, the situation appeared hopeless. But then, an extraordinary phenomenon occurred – The Red Sea parted, enabling the children of Israel to traverse through on dry ground. To understand the essence of faith's resilience portrayed here, we need to delve into the dynamics of this divine intervention.

Firstly, the parting of the Red Sea showed a God who can make a way, where there is seemingly no way. The Israelites were hemmed in between the Red Sea and Pharaoh's chariots racing towards them. They could neither advance forward nor retreat. However, God, in His omnipotence, made a path in the sea. This reminds us that perhaps, the most crucial message we can etch in our minds during dire circumstances is – God can, and He will, make a way.

Secondly, it highlights a God who never abandons His own. Despite their grumblings and complaints against Moses and God himself, the Israelites were never forsaken. His promise to Abraham and Sarah was being fulfilled; their descendants saw the glory of Yahweh in unprecedented ways. This reassures us that despite our fluctuating faithfulness, God's unwavering fidelity endures.

Lastly, the aftermath of the Red Sea parting embodies the absolute and unconditional deliverance offered by God. Pharaoh's army, that was breathing threats and death, was consumed by the sea, leaving not a single one alive. The enemy that you see today, said Moses, you will never see again. Like the Israelites, we can trust God to not only deliver us from our adversaries but to consume and obliterate them.

From these reflections, let's bring this ancient story into our modern context for better understanding:

- When faced with an impasse in life, we should recall God's promise, that He will make a way in the wilderness and rivers in the desert. It is when all human solutions fail, that divine intervention shines brightest.
- God's loyalty is not contingent on our allegiance. Despite our rebellious and selfish inclinations, He never forsakes any that are His. So, we are empowered to stand firm in faith, knowing that God's fidelity is unaffected by our fragility.
- God's deliverance is absolute. The God who did not spare His own Son but delivered Him up for us all, how shall He not also freely give us all things?

In conclusion, the parting of the Red Sea profoundly reveals God's power and fidelity. It paints a vivid image of faith under pressure, responding to divine intervention. We are called to remember, to internalize and to live out these truths - assuring a serene and spiritually strong life, echoing the hope experienced by the children of Israel on that momentous day.

Reflect on the pivotal role of hope and faith during the Red Sea event, as the Israelites battled fear and uncertainty. The colossal rage of the sea ahead, and the wrath of Pharaoh's army behind them, the situation was dire at best. However, imagine the waves of hope and faith that washed over the Israelites, when Moses, under divine providence, parted the waters of the Red Sea. Are we not, today, victims of our Red Seas? Fears and worries that threaten to engulf us, like the tumultuous waves of the mighty sea. And our past, just like the chasing Egyptian army, torments us unrelentingly. What then is our rod of Moses that can make a way where there is no way?

- Perseverance: Much like the Israelites who had to endure a grueling trek through the parted sea bottom, we too must persevere through our trials. Perseverance is our declaration of faith and hope, that we believe a way out exists, even when none is visible.
- Surrender: The Israelites had no army to combat Pharaoh's, no strategy, and no escape route. Their strength lay in their surrender, to a power higher than their collective abilities. Surrender to a divine

plan is not defeat, but an invocation of infinite divine powers working for our betterment.

- Prayer: The Red Sea event was a direct result of divine intervention. This illustrates the power of prayer, an earnest plea from a collective or individual, that can move divine forces to manifest miracles.
- Transformation: The parting of the Red Sea meant a physical journey for the Israelites, but spiritually, it marked a transformational journey. From slavery towards liberation, from oppression towards a promised future. As we navigate our life's Red Seas, each trial is transformative, promising personal growth and spiritual development.
- Gratitude: After their successful crossing, the Israelites sang songs of thanksgiving for their deliverance. Gratitude in times of trial can ease our journey. It shifts our focus from the problem at hand, to the recognition of little blessings that aid us along our path.

In the mirror of ancient texts, we find our reflection. The Bible recounts historical events not as past tales but perennial truths applicable today as they were then. The Red Sea event embodies hope, resilience and spiritual strength that arm us for our life's battles. To delve deep into these stories is to ink our destiny with hope, courage, faith and gratitude, the pillars that form our spiritual strength, the echoes of eternal hope. From slaves to chosen people, the Israelites' journey is symbolic of our life's spiritual journey. Navigating our Red Seas is our way towards our promised land, a place of peace, serenity, and spiritual growth. Each trial reflects a new opportunity for spiritual growth, another chapter in our unique spiritual journey. Just as hope resurfaced for the Israelites, ours too will rekindle, as we part our Red Seas with unwavering faith and resilience.

Journal Exercise:

Reflect on a moment in your life when you were bound by desperation and seemed to face an insurmountable challenge, similar to the Israelites at the Red Sea. Describe your situation in detail, emotions you felt, and the outcome. Now view it through the lens of faith and the miraculous power of God. In what ways can you identify God's interventions during your crisis? How might you act differently in future trials, keeping faith at the forefront? Write down three lessons from this reflection that you can apply to future challenges.

3.3 The Ten Commandments: The Moral Compass

The Ten Commandments, despite their originating in an era far detached from our own, continue to radiate relevance and significance in our modern lives. They serve as a steadfast guide in a time filled with disruption and uncertainty, offering an anchor in the storm of moral debates and ethical challenges. Examining the first commandment, "You shall have no other gods before Me", the central idea is about singularity of faith, about putting God first in all aspects of our lives. Noteworthy, that does not just intrinsically apply to spiritual pursuits, but equally to our priorities in terms of relationships, career, wealth, or personal ambitions. Having God as the compass helps us align our path with righteousness.

Subsequently, the commandment of honoring one's parents serves as an enduring reminder of the importance of respect, obedience, and the recognition of the sacrifices made by those who raised us. It emphasizes nurturing relationships, showing deference, and respecting the wisdom of those who have traversed ahead of us on life's challenging journey. Moreover, the commandment that prohibits false witness urges us to maintain truthfulness, honesty, and accountability in our words and actions. How meaningful would life be if these virtues were genuinely prioritized? This commandment reminds us that being honest and just is not merely about restraint from deceit, but also about promoting fairness, uncompromising integrity, and moral transparency. Meanwhile, the commandments regarding theft and adultery underscore the significance of respect for other people's rights and properties. They suggest that contentment, loyalty and reverence for other's boundaries form the groundwork of a harmonious and equitable society. At last, the commandment 'You shall not covet your neighbor's goods', drives home the point about eliminating greed, envy, and materialistic desires, forces that usually seed unrest and discord. This commandment empowers us to foster gratitude, contentment, and a peaceful mindset.

In essence:

- The Ten Commandments guide us to put God first, before any worldly pursuits.
- They remind us to foster respect, obedience, and gratitude towards our parents and elders.
- Honesty, integrity, and accountability are urged through the admonition against bearing false witness.

- The Commandments underscore respect for others, their rights and properties, promoting an equitable society.
- They teach us to foster gratitude, contentment and peace, steering clear of greed and envy.

So, how do we ensure adherence to these principles in the contemporary world? First one must recognize their significance and the well-rounded growth they foster, not just personally, but at a societal level. Then, it is about cultivating the discipline to live these principles. It's about making conscious choices that reflect the essence of the Commandments, choices that may sometimes challenge prevailing societal norms, but will ultimately lead to an existence that's more harmonious, fulfilling and rooted in deeper spirituality. Boldly yet humbly, allow us to navigate through the sea of wisdom and instruction that resides in the ancient commandments of the bible. Though these commandments were cast thousands of years ago in a context far removed from our modern world, their essence contains timeless truths that hold value across the millenniums. We just have to be open to interpret their central messages in a way that resonates with our present lives.

To begin, let's look at the first commandment: "You shall have no other gods before Me". On first glance, this commandment might seem distant and detached from our 21st-century lives. Most of us, after all, don't worship carved idols or practice archaic religious rituals. But peel back the literal interpretation and you'll find a deeper and more universally applicable principle. You see, 'gods' in this context could be anything we give our time, energy, and devotion to, such as money, status, or pleasure. The central message here is about prioritizing our values, making sure we aren't sacrificing our core ideals for fleeting or less meaningful pursuits.

Another instructive commandment is "Honor your father and your mother." Today, our world thrives on autonomy and individualistic pursuits, often hindering us from understanding and appreciating the wisdom of those who came before us. True, times have evolved and so the dynamics of what constitutes 'honor' have transformed, but the core foundation of respecting and cherishing family bonds and ancestral wisdom remains unchanged.

Let's delve into another commandment - "You shall not steal." The evolution of culture and technology has amplified the nuances of this commandment. 'Stealing' today transcends the physical and ventures into the virtual realm where identities, data, and even ideas can be pilfered. This commandment reminds us to respect others' rights, both in material and intellectual context, compelling us to foster a society based on trust, honesty, and respect.

Each commandment we explore possesses an eternal kernel of wisdom. They call us toward a life of integrity and authenticity; love for our neighbor; respect for life; and a devotion to fairness and justice. Interpreting these age-old commandments in modern context allows us to better understand the obstacles of our times and navigate them with spiritual fortitude, reinforcing our faith's resilience. Pulling back to a bird's-eye-view, reading the commandments as abstract, timeless principles instead of literal, concrete regulations can provide us with a spiritual compass to guide us through our modern journeys. The essence of these commandments functions as a framework, providing us with an inner code of conduct to navigate the complex world we now inhabit.

- ❖ Prioritize our values: The common theme across all commandments is to stay true to our core values over superficial, transient pursuits.
- ❖ Honor our roots: Respect for and connection with our forebears forms a crucial brick in the wall of our personal and collective character building.
- ❖ Respect others' rights: The sacredness of life, property, and personal rights forms the backbone of a moral society and individual integrity.

In the end, drawing out the contemporary relevance of these time-proven commandments not only strengthens our understanding of Scripture but also empowers us with a proactive spiritual toolkit for fostering serenity and spiritual strength. This dynamic interpretation of the commandments puts us at the helm of our spiritual journey, encouraging us to seek transformative understanding and personal growth. It is through this lens, we find the echo of hope resonating through the ages, guiding us toward a life of faith and fortitude.

Commandment Number	Commandment Text	Modern Interpretation
1	You shall have no other gods before Me	Prioritize spiritual values over material possessions
2	You shall not make for yourself an idol	Do not worship material possessions or false idols

Commandment Number	Commandment Text	Modern Interpretation
3	You shall not take the name of the LORD your God in vain	Respect and honor sacred things
4	Remember the Sabbath day to keep it holy	Take time for rest and renewal
5	Honor your father and your mother	Respect and care for elders
6	You shall not murder	Respect all life

In a quest for tranquility, genuine serenity and spiritual vigor, it's fundamental to reflect upon the teachings of the Bible – particularly the Ten Commandments. These divine instructions form an ethical framework that addresses our obligations towards God and others, fostering a peaceful coexistence rooted in respect, empathy and love. We must implement these teachings into our daily existence, embodying their essence beyond mere recitation.

First and foremost, recognizing our dedication to the Creator – 'You shall have no other gods before me' – entails acknowledging the primacy of spiritual virtues over material desires. It demands that we don't idolize wealth, power, or social standing, but instead venerate loftier aspects of the human spirit: kindness, compassion, charity, humility, and perseverance. Our thoughts and actions should echo this devotion, promoting inner peace and nurturing our spiritual strength. Moreover, the commandment 'Honor your father and your mother' encourages respect and love towards our parents, fostering robust familial bonds. But it also extends to elders, educators, and guides in our life. In honoring them, we reinforce mutual respect, patience, and understanding in our interactions, vital ingredients for well-being and societal tranquility.

Honesty is greatly emphasized in 'You shall not bear false witness.' It advocates for truthfulness, not merely in our utterances but also in our actions and intentions. Living a truthful life breeds trust within families, relationships, and communities, strengthening their fabric and fostering serenity within us. To delve deeper into honesty entails shedding pretenses, cultivating authenticity, and aligning our words with our actions, thus, fostering personal integrity and spiritual strength. Furthermore, 'You shall not steal' imbues ethical conduct in regards to possession. It not only condemns physical theft but also intellectual, emotional, and time theft. We should strive to be diligent, respectful of other's efforts, and sincere in our engagements. Applying this commandment in its expanded sense underlines a readiness to do what's right and fair, painting a picture of moral courage that boosts self-esteem and mental tranquility. Respecting boundaries is a pivotal lesson in 'You shall not commit adultery.' It promotes loyalty, faithfulness, and integrity in relationships while connoting an admonition against breaching trust or invasion of personal space. Upholding these values aids in building robust relationships, fostering a sense of emotional security, and garnering inner peace.

Lastly, the most poignant application can be, "You shall not covet." Embracing contentment and gratitude instead of envy and greed leads us to personal peace and satisfaction. It challenges us to appreciate what we have, fostering a culture of gratitude in our minds—leading to spiritual growth and bliss. Applying these commandments in our life means constructing a moral edifice - a temple within us where peace thrives, and spiritual strength flourishes. However, it's not a one-time action; it requires a continuous process of moral self-reflection and self-improvement to truly reap the benefits. Embracing these principles fosters an emotional and spiritual environment conducive to serenity, growth, resilience, and strength. Therefore, as we journey through the chapters of life, let's carry these invaluable Commandments not just in our minds but also in our hearts, practicing their essence in deeds and becoming beacons of hope, resilience, and serenity in today's modern world.

Journal Exercise:

Consider each of the Ten Commandments presented in this chapter. Reflect on how each commandment has played or could play a role in your daily life.

1. Write down one personal practical application for each commandment.
2. For each commandment, describe a situation in which you found it challenging to uphold or when you could have applied it better.
3. Acknowledge one measure you can take in future similar situations to uphold the commandment better.

4. Discuss the impact you perceive the Ten Commandments can have on your interpersonal relationships and spiritual development.

Consider repeating this exercise once every few months, and reflect upon your spiritual journey and personal growth.

4

Wisdom Literature

4.1 Lessons from Job: When Life Doesn't Make Sense

Job, a man of mystifying strength and unwavering faith, faced trials that far surpass those that we can even fathom. Set in the backdrop of the prosperous land of Uz, his cataclysmic narrative of suffering takes center stage providing us with timeless lessons on enduring faith. As we traverse through the turmoil-ridden life of Job, we encounter a man of enviable wealth, profound piety, and utmost integrity. Harmonious furnaces of earth's blessings and heaven's favor molded his fulfilling life. Then, the dreadful storm of adversity struck him, a storm unseen, unfamiliar, unpredictable, unrelenting. Bereft of children, crippled by poverty, abandoned by friends, and afflicted by painful sores, the unimaginable hit Job in wave after wave of relentless trials. What we see isn't just a man ensnared in life's relentless onslaught but also the embodiment of resilience, a beacon of determination illuminating through the deepest abyss of tribulation.

Job's sojourn in the valley of suffering unearths profound truths. The hollowness of suffering breeds understanding, a stark realization that we encounter in his heartbreaking lamentation. But did Job's faith waver in the face of adversity? No. Despite ceaseless suffering, he relentlessly clung unto his Creator, demonstrating perseverance that transcends human understanding. He says in Job 19:25-26 (NIV), "I know that my redeemer lives, and that in the end he will stand on the earth. And after my skin has been destroyed, yet in my flesh I will see God." Here we witness Job's conviction of a divine rescue, a rescue not rooted in expectation but in the essence of stubborn hope mirrored in unbroken faith.

Job's unwavering faith was a testament to a divine unseen. His determination percolated through his lamentations, his queries, and resonates in the tapestry of his enduring spiritual fortitude. His lamentations, unbridled yet faith-filled, served not as chanting of defiance but as echoes of resilience. They were hallowed spaces of genuine surrender, authentic humanity encountering divine mystery. Job's story compels us to take refuge not in the notion of a problem-free life, but in the irreplaceable assurance that our faith, just like Job's, will endure the storm. We too can endure the painful paroxysms of life's adversity, drawing strength not from our power but from the divine within us, echoing the resilience of Job, a man unbroken, unyielding, and undeniably steadfast in his faith. Thus, as we delve into Job's story, let us not merely see a tale scripted in ancient pages but a lived reality carved in faith's resilience. Embrace the storms of life as they come, for these are the tempests that refine us, define us and chisel our faith to radiate resilience and spiritual strength. Indeed, in life's furnace of adversity, the gold of our faith shines brightest.

Lesson Topic	Key Takeaway	Bible Verse
Understanding God's Sovereignty	God's plans are perfect even when they don't align with ours	Job 38:1-18
Job's Endurance	Patience through suffering leads to greater faith	Job 1:21-22
God's Justice	God's justice is beyond human understanding	Job 41:11
God's Grace	God restores Job's fortunes and adds on	Job 42:10
Job's Friends	Listening and consoling are vital during hardships	Job 2:11-13
God's Wisdom	God is all-knowing and man can't contend with that	Job 38:36

As we delve into Job's poignant dialogues, they present an abundant treasure chest of wisdom and insights into the nature of human suffering and divine wisdom. Job's musings are not only a reflection of his pain and desolation but, more profoundly, they are an exploration of life's most profound questions. This exploration is deeply relevant to our present times, enabling us to derive spiritual strength and achieve modern serenity amidst life's tumultuous storms.

Why has God allowed pain and suffering? How should one view this suffering, and how does it relate to our relationship with the divine? These are some of the deeply profound questions that Job grapples with as he takes us on a journey through his dialogues. Through Job's dialogues, we catch a glimpse of his tumultuous internal struggle. His speeches reveal a man grappling to reconcile his faith in an all-powerful, loving God with the harsh reality of his suffering.

At first, he reiterates his innocence and maintains that he has not strayed from the path of righteousness. His anguish compels him to demand an audience with God, to argue his case before Him. We see here a desperate man, someone seeking to understand his plight. This is a struggle that many of us go through when times are tough; it's hard to reconcile our faith with the seemingly random and chaotic nature of life. However, throughout these dialogues, there is a recurring theme—a call for humility in human wisdom. Job's friends offer comforting but conventional wisdom, attributing his suffering to sin. They maintain that if Job would simply repent, his troubles would end. Their view was based on their understanding of God's nature and His justice. In the end, however, this so-called wisdom proves to be an oversimplification of divine wisdom and understanding.

Job's narrative really turns a corner when God responds. God's response to Job is not a direct answer but an invitation to reflect on His works of creation, His sovereignty, and His unfathomable wisdom. Underneath this conversation, the fundamental principle seems to be that human understanding is limited. Despite our best attempts, we will never fully comprehend the mysteries of divine wisdom or the reasons behind our sufferings. Job's humble and steadfast faith, regardless of his circumstances, opens us up to a powerful truth - that resilience of faith does not depend on the absence of questions, doubts, or even anger. It is instead rooted in our relationship with God, a relationship that fosters trust and complete surrender even in the face of inexplicable suffering.

In summary, Job's dialogues shed light on several key insights:

1. The struggle and questioning that come with suffering is a part of the human condition. It's okay to grapple with questions and even to express your confusion to God.

2. It's essential to recognize that divine wisdom is beyond human comprehension. Instead of trying to rationalize suffering, our role is to trust in God's unfathomable wisdom unconditionally.
3. Our friends may offer well-intentioned advice like Job's friends did, but it's important to remember that they don't fully understand the mysteries of God's plans, just like us.
4. Encountering suffering does not necessarily mean you've done something wrong; sometimes, it's a part of a bigger plan that we can't comprehend.
5. The resilience of faith is not about the absence of doubts or questions, but about maintaining a profoundly personal relationship with God, which enables us to surrender to His divine wisdom, irrespective of our circumstances.

Before discussing the transitional arc of this biblical figure, it is noteworthy to highlight that Job's story is a testament to trusting God even when we can't see the end of the journey. Job's unwavering faith in God's wisdom and goodness, even in the midst of immeasurable suffering and loss, is a beacon of hope in times of despair.

Upon stripping Job of his earthly blessings, his so-called 'friends' even began to cast aspersions on his faith and integrity. The heated debates and discussions that ensued, centering around the conventional wisdom of the time, did little to deviate Job from his steadfast trust in God's sovereignty. Instead of harboring resentment and dissatisfaction, Job turn inward for introspection, fostering a space for spiritual growth and maturation. Job's story comes full circle, his prior losses restored twofold when his trials eventually ended, fully demonstrating the recuperative and redeeming power of faith. His amplifying narrative speaks volumes – that God is ever-present, especially in the midst of severe difficulties and trials. This biblical account carries enduring relevance for us. Inside our personal spheres of suffering and disappointment, we might be inclined to question the goodness or wisdom of a higher power. But Job's story encourages us to hold firm, clinging onto our spiritual beliefs against the backdrop of earthly afflictions.

Job's experience and his ultimate restoration underline three essential truths:

1. Suffering and loss are inevitable parts of our earthly lives. Despite the vicissitudes of life, our faith should remain rock solid.
2. God's wisdom and plans are incomprehensible to us. Despite not understanding the reasons for our sufferings, we need to trust that divine wisdom is at work.
3. The power of unwavering faith in God can bring about restitution in ways beyond our comprehension, which encourages us to stand firm even when the season of restoration seems distant.

In times of personal crises and worldwide chaos, the story of Job serves to remind us that faith's resilience extends beyond our temporal understanding. The echoes of hope from these biblical narratives shed light on striking parallels to our contemporary lives, urging us to cultivate an unswerving journey of faith, no matter the trial. It's about seeing beyond our immediate circumstances, always anchoring ourselves in the hope of our divine companionship. The lamentations of today pave the way for the restorations of tomorrow, further underscoring the timeless message in Job's redemptive story. It stands to reason that however turbulent life's sea may be, the anchor of our faith should always be safely lodged in the rock of ages.

Journal Exercise:

Take a moment to look back over the trials and challenges you've faced in your own life. Reflect deeply on the moments where life didn't make sense and seemed unfair, just like Job's experience.

1. Write down one particular circumstance that seemed unbearable at the time.
2. How did you feel in that moment of despair? Describe the emotions you had, using as much detail as you can.
3. How did your faith play a part in this scenario? Did it waver or get stronger?
4. Looking back, can you identify any lessons or areas of growth that came out of this difficult situation?
5. Compare your experiences with Job's. What similarities and differences do you see?

Take this time to think about how your faith might be refined in the future, and reaffirm your trust in God, even in times when life doesn't make sense.

4.2 Proverbs: The Essence of Wisdom

Understanding the Book of Proverbs presents a unique challenge due to its rich symbolism and proverbial sayings. However, a deeper look into this wisdom-filled book reveals timeless lessons that are remarkably relevant to our modern lives. When interpreted within its historical and cultural context, the Proverbs are rich with truth and wisdom. We can glean from them practical direction for everyday living as well as profound theological revelations. Here are some strategies to help interpret and understand the Proverbs:

First, we must recognize the unique literary style of the Proverbs. Unlike narratives or epistles, the Proverbs are filled with metaphors, similes, and other figurative expressions. These are not meant to be read as literal statements; instead, they are symbolic and loaded with meaning. Interpreting the Proverbs requires a keen understanding of their literary style and a willingness to dig deep into the rich imagery they present. Additionally, understanding the original Hebrew language and its nuances can greatly enhance our understanding of the Proverbs. Even if we do not read Hebrew, good study resources can provide us insights into the original language, word meanings, cultural context, and grammatical structures. One particular method that can be applied is the principle of first mention. This is looking for the first occurrence of a word, phrase, or principle in Scripture. Often, the meaning found in that first occurrence carries over into subsequent instances. It's like setting a precedent in court.

Throughout our study, we need to cross-reference other Bible verses and passages. Since Scripture interprets Scripture, looking for similar themes, principles, or word usage in other Bible parts can bring clarity to a particular proverb. Importantly, consider the Proverbs like a mirror to our lives. Each represents wisdom applied to a specific life circumstance. As we pour over these verses, we're meant to see our reflection in them - our behaviors, attitudes, and interactions with others. They are meant to provoke self-evaluation and change. However, it's vitally essential not to canonize a singular Proverb. Recognize that Proverbs provides general truths and guidelines, but it's not a book of promises. In most cases, they describe how life generally works, but they don't predict individual outcomes or guarantee specific results. Lastly, we must spend time meditating on these scriptures. Let them simmer within our hearts and minds. The richness of Proverbs is not easily understood by a cursory read. It requires prayerful consideration and thoughtful meditation.

By taking the time to understand the historical context, literary style, and initial application of the Proverbs, we set the stage for these ancient wisdom gems to spring forth with fresh relevance for our lives today. History is a vast reservoir of wisdom. One cannot overlook the significance of the experiences, philosophies, and guidance that have been preserved in its depths. When we look within the pages of the Proverbs, the book compiles a variation of lived experiences and lessons learned, presented as profound wisdom to guide us. This wisdom has lived through centuries, standing the test of time. As we navigate the challenges of our modern world, let's apply these nuggets of ancient wisdom. One of the prominent teachings of Proverbs concerns the importance of understanding. Proverbs 4:7 underlines, "Wisdom is the principal thing; therefore get wisdom: and with all thy getting get understanding." In other words, wisdom isn't merely about acquiring knowledge but centers around the ability to interpret and apply the knowledge effectively. In today's information era where we are bombarded with news and opinions, let's make it our priority to discern truth and cultivate understanding. Additionally, Proverbs 15:1 shares, "A gentle answer turns away wrath, but a harsh word stirs up anger." Our world is needlessly divided, with hostility simmering beneath the surface of multitudinous societal interactions. This ancient wisdom encourages us to approach our communications with kindness and gentleness, a soft reminder in an era where debates and disagreements can quickly escalate due to a tweet or a media post.

Reliability is another virtue valued in Proverbs. Proverbs 25:19 highlights, "Like a broken tooth or a lame foot is reliance on the unfaithful in a time of trouble." In contemporary society, filled with fickle loyalties and uncertainties, this ancient wisdom underlines the essence of faithfulness and reliability. When forming social or business partnerships, consider the reliability and integrity of your associates. Moreover, Proverbs bolsters individual responsibility. Proverbs 14:23 notes, "In all labor there is profit, but mere talk leads only to poverty." In our modern world of easy shortcuts and instant gratification, genuine hard work can sometimes be undervalued. This proverb prompts us to value and respect the fruit of diligent labor and encourages us to be active contributors to our welfare rather than idle talkers. Lastly, remember the profundity of Proverbs 16:18 - "Pride goes before destruction, a haughty spirit before a fall." Pride can be a blinding force in our lives, preventing us from seeing the reality as it is and leading us down a path of self-destruction. In our accomplishments and successes, let's remain humble, acknowledging that they were not solely our own doing but the result of many unseen forces working in our favor.

These ancient insights encapsulated within Proverbs can guide us as we navigate our complex, modern world. They help us foster meaningful relationships, practice truth in speech and action, value the diligence of hard work, and keep our pride in check, thus nurturing a serene and spiritually strong life. The intricately woven proverbs found in the Holy Bible serve as spiritual nourishment that aids in fostering unshakeable resilience and unending serenity. These instructions, filled with the wisdom of old, help us cultivate a robust faith capable of handling fluctuating life circumstances with grace and fortitude.

When studying the book of Proverbs, we encounter insights illuminating paths to building a resilient faith:

- One would be reminded of Proverbs 3:5-6, "Trust in the LORD with all your heart and lean not on your own understanding; in all your ways submit to Him, and He will make your paths straight." Here, surrendering to divine wisdom results in a deep resilience. Trusting in God translates to letting go of the need to control or understand everything that happens to us. Hence, building endurance even during tumultuous times becomes apparent.
- A snippet of advice from Proverbs 17:22 is also illuminating, "A joyful heart is good medicine, but a broken spirit dries up the bones." This verse signals the importance of spiritual joy in longevity and resilience of life. Joy through faith acts as a restorative balm, healing wounds and strengthening the spirit.
- Proverbs 18:10 divulges, "The name of the LORD is a fortified tower; the righteous run to it and are safe." Implicit within this verse, is the visualization of God as a steadfast refuge in the face of adversity. It accentuates the spiritual strength and security that encompasses those who seek the Lord.

Just as Proverbs guide us in developing resilience, it also paints a picture of peacefulness and serenity that can be accessed through a thriving faith.

- From Proverbs 1:33, it says "But whoever listens to me will live in safety and be at ease, without fear of harm." This scripture tells us that by heeding divine teachings, we bloom in a state of tranquility, free from undue fears and anxieties.

- Proverbs 14:30 conveys the message, "A heart at peace gives life to the body, but envy rots the bones." By submerging our hearts in peace, we cultivate a vivacious and robust life, impervious to the decay brought by envy and resentment.
- Lastly, Proverbs 3:17 explicates, "Her ways are pleasant ways, and all her paths are peace." It shows that walking God's way is synonymous to treading a path strewn with serenity. This sacred peace, is obtainable for all who fully embrace the commands and wisdom that God provides.

Through the perceptive consideration of Proverbs, we unravel the strength within us, tempered by trials and rooted in divine wisdom. More importantly, we encounter the profound serenity that faith offers, a tranquility that runs deeper than fleeting happiness. It's an enduring peace that transcends understanding, a calm that persists despite life's storms. Proverbs offer essential life teachings that instill enduring resilience and serenity within those who are receptive. Therefore, bathing in these sacred guidance enables us to grow in spiritual strength, fostering a faith that is unflinching in the face of adversity and serene amidst the whirlwind of life.

Proverb	Meaning	Culture of Origin
A bird in the hand is worth two in the bush	Securing what you have is better than taking a high risk for more	English
When the cat's away	the mice will play	People will misbehave when they are not monitored
A journey of a thousand miles begins with a single step	Great things start from humble beginnings	Chinese
Fortune favors the brave	Those who are bold or who confront fear or adversity will have better luck	Irish

Proverb	Meaning	Culture of Origin
Two heads are better than one	Two people working together have a better chance of solving a problem than one person working alone	English
The early bird catches the worm	Those who arrive or act first are the most successful	English

Journal Exercise:

1. Take a few moments to identify three key lessons you've gleaned from the Proverbs and write them in your journal.
2. Reflect on how these wisdom insights have already influenced or can influence your daily life. Write a concrete example for each.
3. Identify three challenging situations that you face currently or have recently faced. How can the wisdom from Proverbs be applied to address these situations? Jot down your thoughts.
4. Look at the three lessons you noted earlier. Transform each one into a personal affirmation. Write these in your journal and make a commitment to revisit and reflect upon them each day for the next week.
5. In your own words, describe what wisdom means to you after this chapter. How is this understanding different from what you believed prior to reading about Proverbs?

4.3 Ecclesiastes: The Meaning of Life

As we gaze into the profound depths of Ecclesiastes, we come face-to-face with timeless wisdom that interrogates and explores life's purpose as depicted in the scripture. It unravels profound insights into the human condition, faith, our constant search for meaning, the futility of earthly pursuits, and the inevitability of mortality. More importantly, it provides a framework of spiritual resilience — enduring spiritual muscle cultivated in the crucible of questioning, struggling, and revealed knowledge. Ecclesiastes presents us with a life of limitless pursuits and pleasures, one that seems to only yield emptiness and meaninglessness. In this scripture, we encounter a deeply introspective Solomon, an embodiment of absolute human wisdom and wealth, tirelessly seeking fulfillment in his worldly pursuits. Despite having everything that can be achieved by mortal hands, he proclaims it all as "vanity."

In this context, the word "vanity" does not merely mean conceit or excessive pride. It is a direct reference to the emptiness or hollowness; an encapsulation of the fleeting nature of worldly pursuits and possessions, a transient smoke grasped in vain. For every temporary pleasure, valuable possession, or awe-inspiring achievement, Solomon remarkably concluded, "This too is vanity." From this perspective, Ecclesiastes may seem disheartening, providing a grim outlook on life. But this shadow is not without its silver lining. Solomon urges us not to tether our happiness or joy to material possessions or hollow pursuits. Rather, he beckons us to find ultimate fulfillment and purpose in obeying and revering God. His philosophy can be distilled into a simple truth—God designs every moment of our lives and makes everything beautiful in its time. Understanding this allows us to cherish the joy and beauty in the mundane routines of daily life and realize their integral role in our spiritual journey.

In this myriad of paradoxes and redundancies, we are enlightened on the most vital aspect of our existence: that true wisdom lies not in understanding life's mysteries but in challenging our human-bound rationality and accepting God's inexplicable ways without contest. We are guided to understand that our spiritual strength is not merely gained in seasons of abundance and happiness but also birthed in the crucible of suffering and relentless questioning. In the face of overwhelming unrest, when the fragility of our existence threatens to consume us, Ecclesiastes quietly beckons us to a comforting realization. We are reminded that our lives are not a series of aimless activities, but intricately woven tapestries by a master craftsman, with each thread purposeful, each shade significant. Each rainbow after a spell of rain and each dawn after a dark night serves to affirm, 'This too shall pass.'

By delving deeper into Ecclesiastes, we can uncover how spiritual resilience is not a product of our striving but a fruit of our surrender. It's not achieved, it's received. And once received, it transforms our life lens, enabling us to look at unrest as an opportunity for growth, uncertainty as a breeding ground for faith, and imperfections as reminders of human fragility and God's grace. As we continue to unravel the complexities of the Book of Ecclesiastes, we come across a pivotal theme that reverberates deeply in our lives - perseverance. This concept is not faintly scribbled; it is densely embroidered into the fabric of Ecclesiastes. It asserts that faith, regardless of the direness of the circumstances we face, should always stand firm.

Ecclesiastes teaches that life, like the seasons, is a cyclical process. Everything has its time and season - a time to sow and a time to harvest. Herein lies the first spiritual lesson: It calls us to embrace the ebb and flow of life, with its joys and sorrows, success and failure, life and death. Each time and season challenge us, but each also brings its own unique blessings. Struggles and challenges are merely seasons in our life, moments in time that refine and strengthen our faith before moving on to the next. Another lesson we can extrapolate from the philosophy of Ecclesiastes is its emphasis on temperance. Ecclesiastes cautions against exalting wealth, power, or wisdom as ultimate fulfillment. Instead, it nudges us towards a life of balance and gratitude. Wallowing excessively in the valley of sorrow depletes life of its purpose, and standing too long on the mountain of false illusions can lead us astray. Even in plenty, we must not lose sight of the true meaning of life and real value of faith, emphasizing that 'all is vanity'.

Most notably, however, Ecclesiastes teaches us to have faith in the timing of the divine. It is this lesson of faith's perseverance that is the hardest to master in uncertain times, yet it holds the most valuable key to maintaining spiritual strength. When faced with uncertainty, it's natural to crave answers, to want everything in our control. Ecclesiastes suggests otherwise, encouraging us to trust in the divine's timing and refrain from rushing our lives, declaring "He has made everything beautiful in its time." This doesn't mean we should remain idle, but instead serves to caution us against desperate activities born out of impatience and doubt. When we try to rush our lives, we often miss out on the vital nurturing process that silent waiting imparts. It's through this process that we grow, that our faith is tested and ultimately fortified.

Lastly, Ecclesiastes points out that persistent faith means accepting both the good and bad that life tosses our way. This acknowledgment of life's duality pushes us towards greater spiritual maturity and resilience. A reaffirmation that the dark hours of the night are always met with the promise of dawn. Summing it all up, the insights from Ecclesiastes shine light on faith's perseverance in uncertain times. It's not an easy path to tread, but the beauty of this path is that it leads us to spiritual resilience, equipping us to face the unyielding currents of life with grace, courage, and most importantly, unwavering faith.

Renowned for its poetic elegance and spiritual candidness, the book of Ecclesiastes offers profound wisdom on understanding contentment in the midst of life's inherent transience. One key theme echoed in these biblical texts is the importance of finding satisfaction not in worldly pursuits, but in the divine and the eternal. Though written harking back to antiquated times, these teachings bear implications for contemporary individuals besieged with the pressures and distractions of the 21st century.

Firstly, Ecclesiastes reveals its truth by stating, "Meaningless! Meaningless! Utterly meaningless! Everything is meaningless" (Ecclesiastes 1:2). Yet, this is not a counsel for despair. Rather, it serves to reaffirm our focus on the spiritual, encouraging us to seek gratification not in material gain, professional success, or other transient endeavors, but in striving for spiritual growth and connection with the divine.

Practically applying this teaching in today's context might entail carefully auditing our priorities, and re-evaluating the attention and energy we assign to various areas of our lives. More specifically, it may involve:

- Shifting focus from the observable, material aspects of life to the intangible – empathy, compassion, love, and spiritual growth.
- Regularly reflecting on our life trajectories to identify any unhealthy attachments or dependencies on worldly items or achievements.
- Aligning our actions and decisions in line with our spiritual goals and values, rather than societal expectations or peer pressures.

Secondly, Ecclesiastes eloquently advises, "Whoever loves money never has enough; whoever loves wealth is never satisfied with their income" (Ecclesiastes 5:10). This captures the futility of constantly striving after material wealth and success, which often results in perpetual dissatisfaction and lack of contentment.

In today's context, this wisdom can inform our approach to wealth accumulation and work-life balance. Instead of fixating on monetary gain or professional advancement, we can endeavor to:

- Cultivate a healthy relationship with money, treating it not as the end-goal, but a means to facilitate our spiritual path and other enriching experiences.
- Practice gratitude for what we have, which can help amplify our sense of contentment and serenity amid life's ups and downs.

- ❖ Embrace simplicity, consciously resisting the fast-paced consumerism that often contributes to stress, discontent, and spiritual disconnection.

In conclusion, Ecclesiastes' wisdom encourages us to re-center our lives around the eternal, unerring spiritual path rather than transient, worldly pursuits. This shift in perspective can cultivate a deep-seated serenity and contentment, shielded from the turbulence of modern life. By mindfully applying these teachings, we can tackle the pressures of the contemporary world with strengthened spiritual resilience and grace. Ultimately, we solidify our peaceful relationship with ourselves, the world, and the divine.

Verse Number	Main Theme	Reflection Questions
1.1	Introduction to the Teacher	What do you perceive is the teacher's purpose?
1.2	The meaninglessness of life	How do you personally define the purpose of life?
2.11	The Teacher's reflections on his life	What would you do differently if you had a chance to restart your life?
3.1	The value of time	What is your perception of time and its importance in your life?
4.4	The emptiness of rivalry	How has rivalry impacted your life positively or negatively?
5.10	The vanity of wealth	Do you think wealth can bring ultimate happiness? Why or why not?

Journal Exercise:

List three important lessons or concepts that resonated with you from this chapter on Ecclesiastes: The Meaning of Life. Next to each lesson, write a real world situation where you can apply it. How does understanding Solomon's exploration of the meaning of life guide your own life journey?

Reflect on a time when you felt your life was devoid of meaning or purpose. What perspectives from the Book of Ecclesiastes could have provided you solace during this time?

Rewrite Ecclesiastes 3:1 ("There is a time for everything, and a season for every activity under the heavens") in your own words, and explain how this verse applies in your life right now.

Finally, consider the transient nature of earthly pursuits, as presented in the chapter. In light of these biblical teachings, jot down some ways you can shift your focus to a more eternal perspective on life, building spiritual strength and resilience.

4.4 Psalms: A Spiritual Journey in Verse

Our first expedition into the depths of the Bible's wonderings begins with positioning ourselves in the heart of the 'Psalms'. The book of Psalms, nestled within the centre of the Holy Scriptures, is an anthology of 150 individual hymns, prayers, and poems to God, written by several authors across many centuries. Ranging from the intense highs of divine love to the abyssal lows of human despair, the Psalms serve as spiritual landmarks for us as we endeavor to feel our way through the darkness of our individual voyages. They provide a deep insight into the emotional spectrum of the spiritual journey that we all partake in. Each Psalm is distinct, a unique exploration of the author's relationship with God, humankind, and the wider world. Despite this, they broadly follow themes of praise, thanksgiving, lamentation, and supplication. In our pursuit of spiritual strength, we shall focus on the Psalms of praise. These are not simply about adoring words weighed heavy with gratitude; they reveal the power of faith, the transformative potential of praise, and the resilience it can infuse in our spirits. Among the Psalms of praise, one can discern two subtypes: Descriptive praise and Declarative praise. Descriptive Psalms bring forth a visionary view of God's majesty, illuminating His divine attributes such as His omnipotence, virtue, and mercy. In contrast, Declarative Psalms express gratitude for His deeds, His benevolent acts for His creation — an outright proclamation of trust and thanksgiving for His help and salvation.

Descriptive Psalms, like Psalm 8, offer a profound spiritual insight into God's grandeur juxtaposed alongside human insignificance. It places human beings at the heart of God's creation, underscoring our mandate as stewards of the Earth. Reflecting on such Psalms strengthens our faith by reminding us of the privilege and responsibility that comes with being God's creation. It helps us to better comprehend the loftiness of God and our position in relation to Him.

On the other hand, Declarative Psalms, such as Psalm 66, fill us with hope and gratitude. They recount the wondrous deeds God has performed, stirring up a genuine and spontaneous wave of thanksgiving. These Psalms allow us to appreciate the constant care and guidance God extends towards us, His children. They help us appreciate that hope and faith can thrive even in the most adverse conditions.

However, Psalms of praise aren't merely revelatory; they are transformational. When we meditate upon them and let their words seep into our hearts, they provide motivation to praise God, regardless of our circumstances. They serve as spiritual nourishment, building up our faith's resilience every time we recite them with mindful attention. Ultimately, devoting our time to the Psalms of praise is akin to aligning our spirits with the chorus of faith and thanksgiving that has echoed through the ages. Each verse reinforces our faith, instills tranquility, and fortifies us with an unyielding spiritual strength. Despite the tumult around, we remain grounded, anchored by the vibrant echoes of praise, reverberating within our beings, guiding us ever onwards on our spiritual journey.

Basking in this beautiful chorus of the 'Psalms,' we are ready to venture into the depths of divine wisdom hidden in the Bible's enigmatic narratives.

Psalm Number	Verse Highlight	Interpretation
Psalm 23	"The Lord is my shepherd	I lack nothing"
Psalm 51	"Create in me a pure heart	O God"
Psalm 100	"Shout for joy to the Lord	all the earth"
Psalm 150	"Let everything that has breath praise the Lord"	Expresses the universality of divine praise
Psalm 118	"This is the day that the Lord has made; we will rejoice and be glad in it"	Signifies the reception of each day as a divine gift and a cause for celebration

In the Psalms, expressions of grief range widely, from frank despair to at least partial affirmation of God's faithfulness. This spectrum of sentiments serves as an important tool in growing our spiritual resilience and fostering modern serenity from ancient wisdom. The psalmist treads the valleys of desolation, expressing the depths of human suffering, yet seeking to retain faith amidst the despair. Drawing from the Psalms, let us connect these profound expressions with modern realities as a means to navigate our own valleys of desolation. To begin with, we turn to Psalm 22, where we feel the psalmist's utter despair: "My God, my God, why have you forsaken me?" The despair depicted here is total and disturbing, speaking openly to emotions many of us grapple with at some point in life. It's crucial to remember, however, that expressions of despair are bred not from a lack of faith, but from steadfast faith clashing with harsh realities. Even in the depths of suffering, the psalmist pushes us to question, to seek understanding and refuge in what is immovable – our foundational faith.

Next, consider Psalm 88, the darkest of the Psalms. This Psalm opens with a plea: "O Lord, God of my salvation, I cry out day and night before you," and ends with a stark, "darkness is my closest friend." While this lament seems void of any hopefulness, it indeed accomplishes a paramount purpose: conveying the reality of suffering without censorship or sugar-coating. It articulates to us that it's human and natural to grieve and allow our feelings to flow freely. Suppressing these sentiments can harm our spiritual and emotional wellbeing.

Lastly, let us examine Psalm 77, where we observe a significant turn from despair to a muted hope. The psalmist, even amidst the storm of his sorrows, pauses to reflect upon the deeds of God: "I will remember the deeds of the Lord; yes, I will remember your wonders of old." It teaches us that even when the current tide of troubles threatens to overpower us, we can choose to remember past victories, reminding ourselves of the wonders God has done in our lives and therein find a glimmer of hope.

The Psalms, in all their raw honesty and emotional intensity, are not just a collection of ancient songs but an intimate reflection of our collective human experience. Indeed, faith and grief are not mutually exclusive. It's in acknowledging and expressing our pain, our doubts, and our fears that we carve pathways to a deeper relationship with God and discover extraordinary resilience. Through these chapters of Psalms, we learn that it's okay to question, to cry, to be weary. We learn that pain and suffering are as real as joy and victory, and they serve an equally instrumental role in our spiritual journey. When viewed in this way, the echoed grief in the Psalms helps us foster a strengthened relationship with God, nurturing our faith to be more resilient amid adversities of life. Throughout the Psalms, the theme of hope and redemption is resounding and potent. These words that have been echoed through centuries of faith, have served travelers on their spiritual journey as a guiding star, illuminating a path through even the darkest seasons of desolation.

In understanding the intertwining themes of hope and redemption within the Psalms, it is essential to recognize the purpose of these ancient songs. They were not composed with the mere intention of musical expression; instead, they were crafted as raw, emotional pleas to openly express personal grief, tumultuous doubt, and boundless joy. Whenever life presented a situation that seemed inscrutable, the authors would pour their sentiments into the verses of the Psalms. This vulnerability created a spiritual safe space for expressing even the harshest feelings of abandonment or despair.

One quintessential example of the soaring theme of hope in Psalms is Psalm 42, where the author complains about being persecuted and wonders why God has seemingly abandoned him. Yet, despite his deep melancholy, he holds onto hope, declaring, "Why, my soul, are you downcast? Why so disturbed within me? Put your hope in God, for I will yet praise him, my Savior and my God" (Psalm 42:5). This verse reveals two powerful insights:

1. Hope is a deliberate choice: Despite feeling desolate and abandoned, the author chooses to hope in God. This teaches us that hope is not a circumstantial emotion, but a willful decision we can opt for, regardless of our situations.
2. Hope is grounded in faith: The author identifies God as his Savior, indicating his firm faith in God's ability to deliver him from his predicament. This underscores the importance of faith as the foundational bedrock of hope.

Turning our attention to the theme of redemption in Psalms, Psalm 103 beautifully encapsulates this divine principle. It begins with personal praise but soon expands to celebrate God's gracious acts towards all who turn to Him. In verse 4, the author says, "who redeems your life from the pit and crowns you with love and compassion". This powerful verse highlights crucial aspects of redemption:

3. God initiates redemption: It is God who pulls us out from the depths of despair and renews our lives. This reiterates the essential role of divine intervention in the process of redemption.
4. Redemption is a transformative process: The verse suggests a two-fold transformation - removal from despair, and an elevation to a position of love and compassion. This emphasizes how redemption can fundamentally alter our spiritual state and improve our life condition.

The study of hope and redemption in the Psalms serves to remind us of the echo of divinity in every trial we face. It calls us to cultivate an attitude of trust and relentless optimism, engendered by a buoyant hope in God's divine plan for our lives. Even in times of distress and chaos, these Psalms encourage us to ascend triumphantly, carried aloft on the wings of redemption, stepping into the abundant future God has prepared for us.

Journal Exercise:

1. Reflect on a verse from the Psalms that particularly resonated with you in this chapter. Write it down and beneath it, jot down why it stirred your spirit.
2. Psalms consist of prayers, praises, and lamentations. Choose one theme and pen down a brief psalm of your own. Express yourself sincerely, as if it is a heartfelt conversation with God.
3. Think about the elements in Psalms that make it spiritually nourishing for you. Identify these elements and note down how you can incorporate such aspects into your daily spiritual routine or prayer life.
4. Imagine yourself in the situations that the Psalmist was in when they wrote their psalm. How does that change your perspective on the psalms and their relevance to your life? Reflect on this and record your insights.
5. The Psalms speak into both seasons of joy and seasons of difficulty. Recollect a personal experience that reminded you of a Psalm read in this chapter. Journal your thoughts and emotions from that moment and how reading the Psalm now impact that memory.

Remember, this is your personal space. There is no right or wrong answer, take your own time and let your thoughts flow freely.

5
Major Prophets

5.1 Isaiah: Visions of Hope and Judgment

In those days, Isaiah served in the court of King Uzziah, gathering wisdom and navigating the political tides. Then one day, in the year of King Uzziah's death, he found himself in the heavenly throne room, an impossible sight, seen only by rare visionaries. This moment marked the shift from a silent observer to an active participant in the grand scheme of divine plans. Isaiah saw the Lord high and lifted up, the train of His robe filling the temple. Above Him were heavenly beings, seraphim, each with six wings, their voices shaking the doorposts and thresholds. They called to one another, "Holy, holy, holy is the Lord of hosts! The whole earth is full of His glory." Consumed by the divine spectacle, Isaiah felt an irresistible pull, a profound call into the extraordinary.

However, Isaiah's first response felt far from heroic, indeed almost anticlimactic. He lamented, "Woe to me! I am lost, for I am a man of unclean lips, and I dwell in the midst of a people of unclean lips." The disparity between the divine grandeur and his earthly limitations were overwhelmingly apparent. Yet, even in his self-imposed exile, Isaiah witnessed the mercy of the Lord. A Seraphim angel touched his lips with a live coal taken from the altar, purging his sin and relieving his guilt. This holy cleansing prepared Isaiah for what came next.

Now unburdened, Isaiah was addressed directly by the Lord, "Whom shall I send, and who will go for us?" To this collective inquiry, Isaiah unabashedly stepped forward and declared, "Here I am! Send me." Remarkably, Isaiah's response not only embodied submission but also demonstrated proactive willingness, a trait characteristic of the stalwarts of faith. Isaiah's vision illuminates essential facets for understanding and interpreting prophetic visions. Three key takeaways include:

1. The Role of Divine Revelations: Prophetic visions offer glimpses into God's realm, unveiling divine truths and exposing moral deficiencies. These revelations serve to promote humility, inspire repentance, and set the course for personal as well as communal transformations.
2. The Process of Purification: Often the first step toward understanding a divine mission is acknowledging one's own weaknesses or inadequacies. It's through paradoxical admittance of our limitations that we become eligible for divine enablement. God's mercy doesn't ignore our inadequacies; rather it seeks to purge and purify us, as depicted in Isaiah's purification by the seraphim.
3. Readiness for the Divine Call: Once prepared, the individual is presented with a divine assignment. This follows the principle of divine-human partnership that God uses ordinary people, once prepared, to carry out His extraordinary plans. Isaiah's ready acceptance of the divine call demonstrates the courage and commitment to echo the divine will.

By examining Isaiah's distinct spiritual awakening, we gain profound insights into God's intentions for humanity. The vision of Isaiah brings into sharp perspective the divine-human communication, reminding us of the resiliency of faith and our situations within a larger, divine narrative.

Making our way into the prophetic revelations of Isaiah, we encounter a scenery laid out for an ancient class in faith's endurance and hope's pertinacity. Isaiah's prophetic scripture briskly leads us into a parti-colored spectrum of robust judgment intermingled with the harmonious hues of covenantal promise and glorious redemption - echoes of hope persisting through the veil of chastisement. The commencement of Isaiah's visions is inundated with severe judgment against Judah's rebellious ways. God's righteousness demands this chastisement, but His enduring love obliges redemption. Vibrant echoes of hope persist in the backdrop, much like dawn persisting amid the thickest night.

The metaphorical message of hope is robustly evident in Isaiah 6:13. Despite the terrifying vision of near-total destruction, where only a "tenth remains", the Sycomore stump represents resilient faith and God's covenant promise. A spiritual sprouting through the stump speaks to God's unwavering intention for His people's rebirth; His divine business of redemptive restoration is never dormant, even in moments of divine judgment.

Take note of two noticeable attributes in Isaiah's vision:

A. The overwhelming extent of the judgment did not signify complete annihilation; rather, it served to purify and restore a remnant to divine obedience. Judgment and promise were intertwined - purging, preparing, and polishing Judah for a time of spiritual flourishing.

B. The sycomore stump, a humble yet vivid illustration of resilience, was far from dead or past hope. Even in times of utter disarray, God's spirit of hope lingers. The divine promise of rebirth precedes the physical manifestation of restoration.

In the 11th chapter, faith's resilience is further amplified as the Messiah is prophetically depicted as a shoot springing from the Jesse stump, bringing forth unprecedented peace and righteousness. The redemption promise here underscores the power of faith and hope, transcending beyond human comprehension or historical precedence, extending even unto the animal kingdom.

Awesome as Isaiah's visions are, they do not merely belong to an ancient world, but ring true in our times, and will continue to do so in future ages. Indeed, Isaiah's revelations are designed for our introspection, to steel us in spiritual strength, fostering an undying hope, even in the face of looming judgment.

Understanding these Urim-lit patterns within God's Word are crucial for:

1. Trusting in God's sovereignty, regardless of looming judgment or hardship.
2. Upholding resilient faith, and recognizing the interplay of divine judgment and redemption.
3. Keeping hope alive, knowing that even amid trial and tumult, God is engineering our spiritual rebirth and redemption.

So, as we deep-dive into the profundities of faith resilience depicted through these biblical visions, we must allow them to echo in our hearts, stirring within us a surging tide of modern serenity and spiritual strength. Each echo a testament of the relentless hope amid judgment, and our divine calling to live, love, and lead in the rhythm of this eternal melody. As we journey through scripture, we delve deeper into the intricate life of Isaiah, marked by unyielding faith and unparalleled resilience. It is from these rich Biblical narratives that we gather precious nuggets of wisdom, powerful enough to transform the landscape of our modern spiritual lives. By embracing the most difficult moments of his life as opportunities for growth, Isaiah provides an enduring model for us. His resilience is not born out of brute strength or stubborn resisting, but from a deep and abiding faith, an unwavering commitment to trust in God, no matter the circumstance. How do we apply this in our contemporary lives? How do we learn from Isaiah's faith, cultivating our spiritual strength and serenity?

When faced with hardship, Isaiah leaned into his faith, trusting God's plan even during times of uncertainty and despair. He understood that faith was not merely a spiritual crutch but a robust tool of resilience. Understanding this foundational lesson can be transformative in our lives as well. In moments of darkness, we are not called to be simply stoic or cheerful, but patient and bathed in prayer, holding fast to faith even in the face of adversity. Through consistent prayer and meditation, we can welcome serenity into our lives amidst the storm. Isaiah's life also underscores the importance of unwavering obedience to God. Despite Isaiah's circumstances, he never allowed his faith to falter. Instead, he trusted in divine providence. This remarkable display of obedience allowed Isaiah to bounce back from hardship after hardship. Similarly, in our spiritual journey, obedience brings fortitude. Practicing routine spiritual exercises such as reading Scriptures, prayer, and guided meditations can allow us to remain obedient to God's word, strategically preparing us for life's storms before they even arrive.

Moreover, Isaiah was deeply rooted in hope, allowing him to remain at peace despite the turmoil that raged around him. When threats encircled him, he found solace in the promises of God, intertwining warmth into the fabric of his resilience. This invaluable lesson is often overlooked in our quest for spiritual growth. But, by cultivating hope in our lives, we can build a resilience that keeps us grounded during life's storms and grants us momentary glimpses of serenity even in our darkest hours. Isaiah's resilience in faith is not an abstract concept buried within the layers of ancient Biblical text, but a living truth with real-world implications. In unpacking these lessons, we're awakening to a call - a call to manifest resilience, to cultivate spiritual strength, and foster serenity.

These lessons do not act as mere suggestions, but as crucial components in our quest for a fulfilling spiritual life. As we strive to become more like Isaiah in our modern lives, we are drawing from an ancient well of wisdom that enriches our journey of faith. As we echo Isaiah's resilience of faith, we strengthen our spiritual muscles, paving the way for a faith capable of withstanding the waves of life. Just as Isaiah underlined the importance of submission to God, we too must surrender, opening our hearts to divine intervention. Lastly, by embracing a spirit of hope, we bolster our resilience, deepening our faith, and enhancing our emotional serenity.

Verse Number	Message Theme	Significance
1	God's Call to Isaiah	Isaiah's divine commission
5	The Vineyard Song	Critique of the people's unfaithfulness
6	Isaiah's Vision of the Lord	Depiction of God's holiness
9	The Sign of Immanuel	Promise of divine assistance
13	Burden of Babylon	Foretelling of future judgment
23	Oracle Concerning Tyre	Prophecy about the downfall of powerful cities

Journal Exercise:

Pause for a moment and recall the visions described in this chapter. How do they resonate with your personal experiences and your current understanding of the world? Write about a situation in your life where you saw echoes of hope amidst judgment. How did those experiences shape your faith? Now, envision an instance in the future where you could apply the teachings of Isaiah for spiritual strength and serenity.

5.2 Jeremiah: A Prophet's Tears

Jeremiah's calling as a prophet was by no means a walk in the park. In his book, Jeremiah laid out his laments, casting light not only on the emotional burden that befell him but also the reality of being entrusted with a prophetic calling. While God provided him with divine revelations, Jeremiah still remained a human, susceptible to the emotional turmoil brought about by his prophetic role. One of the most poignant aspects of Jeremiah's lament is his profound sense of loneliness. Despite being graced with divine insight, he was met with hostilities and scorn from those around him. They resisted his calls to reform and viewed him as a harbinger of bad news rather than a messenger of divine will. He felt isolated, distanced from his community because of his divine mandate, a bitter pill to swallow for someone tasked with guiding them.

In Jeremiah's lament, there is also an echo of deep agony over the state of his nation. Charged with pronouncing judgment over the disobediences of his people, his role seemed to amplify his anguish and despair. He was a man in love with his nation, witnessing its imminent decay from the sidelines. His pain was a manifestation of his compassion, making his words not simply those of a divine overseer but a man authentically wrestling with the complexities of his prophetic calling. Jeremiah's story also embodies the tension of faith and doubt, a struggle humanity navigates even today. Mourning the impending doom of his nation, Jeremiah also questioned God. He wondered aloud why the wicked prospered while the righteous suffered, a dilemma echoing the heart of every believer who has ever questioned the seemingly contradictory nature of divine justice. His honesty presents a comforting narrative that it is okay for faith to be a struggle.

From Jeremiah's laments, we are handed a raw example of what it truly means to hold a prophetic calling. Among his cries, we find a man torn between his love for his nation and his dutiful allegiance to God. The reality of the prophetic calling is not without hardship, pain, and even doubt. However, through his trials and tribulations, Jeremiah also showcased his unwavering resilience. Demonstrating that even in the harshest of times, it is possible to hold onto faith and hope, thereby personifying spiritual strength of the highest order. Jeremiah's prophetic revelations provide a clear testament as to the divine messages that can surface even amidst despair. At a time when Jerusalem was besieged, and moral degradation was evident, Jeremiah continued to receive divine prophesies, making him the beacon of faith resilience. Delving deep into this compelling narrative is integral to understanding how to apply these teachings in contemporary settings. Admittedly, the circumstances we face today might differ significantly from the siege of Jerusalem, but the essence of the trials remains. We often find ourselves in situations where despair seems pervasive, where the path appears lost. And it is here that Jeremiah's prophetic revelations become crucial.

At the height of the suffering, when the future seemed devoid of hope, Jeremiah witnessed a prophesy, not one of doom, but a prophesy of a future of hope and restoration. The divine revelation resonated the themes of assurance and deliverance, "For I know the plans I have for you," declares the Lord, "plans to prosper you and not to harm you, plans to give you hope and a future" (Jeremiah 29:11, NIV). This prophetic message, midst monumental despair, embodied the boundless realm of God's compassion.

Contemplating the divine revelations from multiple perspectives can illuminate one's life:

- First, acknowledging there's no despair devoid of hope. Every bit of darkness bears a spark of divine light within it. Jeremiah's prophetic revelations came at the peak of Judah's despair. However, its content was brimming with the promise of a bright future, reaffirming that even within profound tribulations, God continues to work in mysterious ways.
- Secondly, understanding God's timing is paramount. Jeremiah's prophetic message brought hope, but it did not warrant an immediate end to the trials. Instead, it promised deliverance in God's specific time, reminding us that without the darkness, one cannot appreciate the light. Navigating the storms of today with the conviction of a brighter tomorrow fuels spiritual resilience, enriching faith in God's perfect timing.
- Finally, cultivating active faith amidst adversity. Jeremiah's faith did not sway under the dire circumstances. His trust remained steadfast, projecting a fundamental lesson - faith is not just about accepting God's gifts but also about holding the line when the tide turns.

The detailed examination of Jeremiah's prophetic revelations imparts valuable lessons on continuing faith amidst despair. Through an accurate reading and comprehension of these narratives, one can build the fortitude to face adversities courageously, fostering faith resilience, and achieving serenity in the present and strength for encounters in the futures yet to unfold. The echoes of hope that reverberate from Jeremiah's story serve to engage and inspire, transforming understanding and shaping how we live out our faith in a modern world.

Verse Number	Verse Content	Verse Discussion
1	"The word that came to Jeremiah"	Discussion of Verse 1
2	"'Thus speaks the LORD'"	Discussion of Verse 2
3	"And I have filled him with the spirit of God"	Discussion of Verse 3
4	"In wisdom and understanding	and in knowledge"
5	"And in all manner of workmanship"	Discussion of Verse 5

In examining the last recorded years of Jeremiah's life, he remained an incorrigible cornerstone in the court of kings - a man bound by duty to relay God's guidance, even amidst a hostile leadership that preferred the blindness of pride over the humbling wisdom of the divine. How he faced his trials holds lessons as responses to the struggles of the modern faith. Consider these essential takeaways from Jeremiah's narrative that inspire resilience, serenity, and spiritual strength in the relentless tide of today's faith challenges:

- The Might of Honest Prayer: Jeremiah, like numerous dedicated believers, tasted periods of intense disdain, disillusionment, and depression. Yet, he found strength in prayer—he communicated his deepest doubts, fears, and complaints – to God. This sincerity in prayer is a blueprint for us, reminding us that God welcomes open hearts, even embattled with concerns or skepticism.
- Placing God's Will Before Personal Gain: At great personal risk, Jeremiah consistently prioritized the will of God over his own safety and comfort. Even facing imprisonment, he courageously pronounced God's revelation in the face of hostility. This tenacity serves as a strong reminder to believers that sometimes, the path of righteousness might lead through the darkest valleys, but the faithful should never lose hope nor shirk their duty.
- Perseverance through adversity: Jeremiah's life was a trail of trials. However, his faith and courage remained unbroken. Instead of succumbing to despair, he found peace and strength in his unfaltering faith in God's justice, even enduring years of captivity.

This spirit of perseverance resonates with modern believers, face to face with their burdens, urging them never to surrender to adversity but to find resilience in faith.

- ❖ Prophet of Hope – Jeremiah's fears and complaints never eclipsed his role as a vessel of hope. Amid his ominous warnings, he prophesied the New Covenant, God's promise of a hopeful future. Contemporary believers must remember that faith encompasses more than the immediate challenges—it is the torch illuminating the path to a divinely ordained future, unmarred by today's transient tribulations.

Jeremiah's enduring faith higher the evident fulfillment of his prophecies make him an apt subject for modern contemplation, especially in a world where faith faces varied trials daily. Applying the lessons from his life teaches us to remain hopeful, resilient, and spiritually strong. Personal struggles may momentarily veil our path, but God's eternal promise of redemption echoes louder than life's transient tribulations. Remarkable faith is not about evading trials but enduring them, armed with our unyielding belief and God's enduring love.

In this chapter, we discovered the lessons from the life of Jeremiah, which still influence and steer us towards spiritual growth. The narratives of biblical heroes like Jeremiah are not historical footnotes; instead, they echo the resilient spirit of faith, offering a treasure-chest of wisdom and guidance for those seeking serenity amidst life's inevitable trials.

Journal Exercise:

Reflect on Jeremiah's suffering and resilience in the face of persecution. How do you see these moments in your own life where hardships have tested your faith? Write about a time when you felt like Jeremiah; alone, misunderstood, or ignored. How did your faith help you withstand? How did it grow? Jeremiah wept for his people, yet never lost hope in God's promises. Are there instances in your life or in the world today that cause you to weep, questioning God's plan? How do your 'tears' turn into seeds of hope?

5.3 Daniel: Integrity in Exile

Daniel, the prophet, serves as a powerful vessel for demonstrating fortitude and resilience in faith, borne from the divine inspiration sourced from

Yahweh. His dramatic life was composed of a distinct tapestry of trials and tribulations, culminating in the iconic narrative of his survival in a den of lions. Despite his disheartening circumstances, with the likelihood of death looming large, Daniel's unwavering faith and consistent prayer life remained intact. Among the narrative's many lessons, the aspect of resilience in faith stands at the forefront. However, this resilience wasn't born out of thin air. It was cultivated and fortified through a myriad of spiritual and practical habits. These included regular prayer, devotion to God's law, and an unshakeable trust in divine providence.

First, the regularity of Daniel's prayer life was a pinnacle of his spiritual practice. Despite knowing that his prayers could potentially lead to his death, he remained undeterred. This courageous act was not simply about defying an unjust law, it was a manifestation of a deeply rooted belief that continuous communication with God was essential for life. It was a testament of resilience that flew in the face of mortal danger.

Second, Daniel's commitment to God's laws served as a reminder of the role of discipline in the cultivation of spiritual resilience. By consciously choosing to uphold these laws even when they went against the norms of the foreign culture he was immersed in, he demonstrated a steadfastness in faith that transcended his immediate surroundings. This unwavering commitment was indicative of his psychological resistance to being swayed by external influences that could lead to spiritual compromise.

Third, implicit in the story of Daniel in the lion's den, is his trust in divine providence. A trust that was neither passive nor fatalistic, but rather active and hopeful. By voluntarily walking into the den, and emerging unscathed, he exhibited the profound belief that God was actively involved in his life, guiding his steps, and providing a way where there seemed to be none. Such faith undeniably required a tremendous level of spiritual strength and resilience.

To translate these spiritual practices into our modern lives, we need to focus on maintaining a continuous dialogue with God, even when life's pressures attempt to push us away. We need to make a conscious effort to abide by God's Word, even when it seems impractical or inconvenient. And we need to remember God's omnipresence in our lives, allowing that understanding to solidify our faith amid trials and tribulations. Like Daniel, let's allow these practices to create an echo of hope in our lives, emanating resilience that can withstand the harshest of tests. When one considers the biblical events involving figures transcending unfamiliar territories, one soon realizes the immense strength of their integrity. In some situations, it was faith that helped these individuals maintain their moral and ethical spinal cords when they were in foreign lands, diametrically opposite to their habitual environments. These stories provide powerful lessons about resilience, personal strength, and the power of integrity.

Perhaps one of the most remarkable instances of this unyielding integrity unfolding in an unfamiliar territory can be found in the story of Joseph, son of Jacob. Sold into slavery by his envious brothers, Joseph found himself in Egypt, miles away from his familiar environment. Yet, despite the harsh and alien conditions, Joseph strongly stuck to his values. Joseph's perseverance and humility were tested on multiple occasions, but he remained firm in his integrity, rejecting Potipar's wife's seductive advances and staying true to his moral compass. His unwavering integrity and commitment to his virtues won him favor in the eyes of the Pharaoh, eventually ascending to the rank of governor, second only to the Pharaoh himself.

Another impactful tale of integrity in a foreign land involves the story of Daniel in Babylon. Brought to Babylon after the defeat of his nation, Daniel quickly made a place for himself in the king's court. However, he never let his new position or environment corrupt his moral judgment. His commitment to his religious principles was tested when the king enacted a law prohibiting prayers to anyone except the king. Nonetheless, Daniel chose to disobey the law rather than compromise his faith, exuding immense resilience and a tenacious grip on his principles.

These stories demonstrate several core virtues that we can aim to assimilate in our lives:

- Perseverance: Both Joseph and Daniel were subjected to circumstances that could have easily deterred them from their faith. But they persevered, providing us a powerful model of resilience in the face of adversity.
- Humility: Despite their eventual high rankings, both Joseph and Daniel remained humble. Their stories remind us that irrespective of our status, it's crucial to stay grounded and be true to our roots.
- Courage: Joseph and Daniel stood up for their faith, displaying immense courage. They inspire us to have the bravery to stand up for our beliefs, even when they're not in agreement with the conventional wisdom or laws.

- Integrity: Perhaps the most significant lesson from these stories is that of integrity. Whether it was Joseph refusing Potipar's wife or Daniel insisting on praying to his God, these titans of faith stood firm.

In conclusion, individuals of faith can find resilience in these ancient stories for their modern serenity. By examining the lives and decisions of these biblical figures, we can learn to invigorate our spiritual strength and take heart when facing adversity or making tough decisions. The echoes of hope reside in these historical accounts, presenting us timeless principles and exhibiting the incredible strength of integrity even in foreign lands.

Verse Number	Key Event	Reflection
1	Arrival in Babylon	Importance of resilience
2	Interpretation of Dream	Dedication to truth and wisdom
3	Appointment to high office	Result of hard work and honesty
4	Refusal to worship the golden image	Commitment to faith and principles
5	Interpretation of the writing on the wall	God's judgment is inescapable
6	Survival in the lion's den	Trust in God's protection

Our journey into the spiritual resilience embedded in Bible narratives brings us to the exploration of dreams and visions, which played pivotal roles as means of divine communication. Resonating with the theme of Faith's resilience, ponder on the life stories of Abraham, Joseph, and Daniel - each of whom experienced dreams and visions as conduits of prophetic revelations from God.

Envision Abraham, a man of Faith, being promised innumerous descendants as he gazed upon the night sky strewn with glittering stars - a vision that became a foundation for Abrahamic religions. While the fulfillment of God's promise seemed improbable due to Sarah's barrenness, Abraham held steadfast in his faith. He understood that God, in His sovereignty, was not confined to operating within the bounds of human understanding. Joseph, the favored son of Jacob, had dreams that later shaped not only his destiny but also the future of the entire nation of Israel. Sold into slavery by his brothers, Joseph's faith in God remained unshaken. He trusted that the dreams he had as a young boy were God-given visions of his future. His unwavering faith in God even in tumultuous times speaks volumes about the resilience of his faith.

Similarly, Daniel's supernatural interpretation of King Nebuchadnezzar's dream led to his prominence in the Babylonian court. The Sovereign hand of God was evident, as Daniel could unravel the King's dream only by divine revelation. Trusting in God enabled Daniel to find favor in the eyes of the King and invariably preserved the lives of the wise men of Babylon. Certainly, dreams and visions demand discernment. We may be tempted to dismiss them as figments of our imagination. However, the Bible teaches that they have potential to be catalysts for divine influence in our lives.

The stories of these prophetic dreamers encourage us as believers to:

1. Understand that God, in His infinite wisdom, may choose to communicate with us through dreams and visions, revealing His will and His direction for our lives.
2. Believe beyond the logical confines of human reasoning, bearing in mind that our faith is grounded in a God who exceeds human comprehension.
3. Maintain resilience in our faith, remembering that divine visions may take time to manifest, just as they did in the lives of Abraham, Joseph, and Daniel.
4. Trust in God's sovereignty, acknowledging that He can overrule our circumstances to bring about His divine plans, as exemplified in the joyous destinies that unfolded for our biblical protagonists.

As we allow these lessons to penetrate deeply into our spirits, we not only gain spiritual strength but also a renewed serenity in the understanding of God's special ways of communication, and His majestic and inexplicable sovereignty. Through dreams and visions, God breathed hope into the lives of the faithful and beckoned them to trust Him.

In conclusion, take comfort in knowing that God is the author of your life story. Whether He chooses to guide through dreams and visions or through other means, the resilience of our faith lies in surrendering to His sovereignty, and in fully trusting that His plans for us will always lead to our ultimate good in His perfect timing. Let these narratives become echoes of hope, that strengthen and embolden your faith, propelling you towards spiritual serenity and strength in the modern world.

Journal Exercise:

Reflect on the life of Daniel as portrayed in the chapter. Consider his commitment to his faith, even when surrounded by a foreign culture and under the threat of persecution. How does his story resonate with you? Write about a time when you had to stand up for your beliefs and maintain your integrity, even when it was challenging. What did you learn from that experience and how can you apply this lesson to your current life situation?

Now, take a moment to think about an aspect of your life where you have been compromising your integrity or deviating from your faith. Ask yourself why you are doing this and how you can find the strength to return to your convictions in this area. Write a commitment to yourself detailing how you plan to uphold your integrity henceforth. Use Daniel's resilience as inspiration for guiding your course of action.

Lastly, pen down a prayer asking for strength, wisdom, and fortitude to remain true to your beliefs, just as Daniel did -- regardless of external pressures.

5.4 Ezekiel: The Spiritual Watchman

Born into a spiritually devout family from the priestly cadre, the life journey of Ezekiel makes an enchanting tale of fidelity, faith, and fortitude. His story unfolds in the backdrop of tumultuous times, when his homeland, Judea, was a vassal state under the oppressive Neo-Babylonian Empire. His own life was marked with the pangs of bondage as he, along with a multitude of compatriots, was forcibly relocated during the second Diaspora. Yet, amid such desolation, the young priest found his unique calling to be a voice of the Divine. Ezekiel was more than a religious figure. His role transcended the mere duties of a priest. It was the profound experiences that he encountered whilst in exilic captivity that fashioned him into an astute visionary, a prophesier, and most importantly, God's appointed watchman. What made this role particularly crucial was the timing - the nation was at low ebb, its people disoriented and disheartened, the future seemingly bleak.

In opposition to this gloomy backdrop, it was Ezekiel's revelations that offered a glimmer of hope. The content of his prophecies was largely symbolic, often represented through vivid and complex imagery. This characteristic style of communication in many ways added a deeper, more existential dimension to his teachings and harbingers. His realization of God's message for his people, therefore, was not limited to mere foreseeing of events; it set the foundation of a new spiritual understanding of their relationship with God. Ezekiel emerged as the sentinel at this critical juncture, assigned with the task of offering hope to a beleaguered nation on the one hand, and serving as a stern reminder of their divine commitments on the other. He was to keep a vigilant watch and deliver God's messages, both of retribution for their collective digressions and of the promise of future restoration. His life and mission thus underlined the divine confluence of justice and mercy: the loving God who punishes to restore rather than to repress His wayward children.

Ezekiel's life can be summarized in the following ways:

- Ezekiel, God's chosen vessel: From an ordinary priest to a chosen instrument of God, the transformational journey of Ezekiel stands testament to the divine power that selects its own instruments and equips them to fulfill their preordained missions.
- Ezekiel, the visionary prophet: His prophecies, rich in symbols and hidden truths, shed new light on God's plans for His people. Ezekiel envisioned a God devoid of geographical limitations, a God whose righteous judgment and merciful restoration extended beyond the boundaries of their homeland.
- Ezekiel, the watchman: His role as the divine watchman set him apart. Tasked with relaying God's messages of retribution and restoration, Ezekiel bore the responsibility of guiding and warning his people.

Therefore, the story of Ezekiel reinforces the power of faith and resilience in the midst of adversity. His role as God's watchman underlines the possibility of hope and spiritual strength that can be elicited even amidst the bondage of exile, the echoes of which still inspire us today.

In the book of Ezekiel, we find that the form of prophecy embraced is not the casual everyday language, but a unique and profound form of symbolic speech. This is well exemplified by Ezekiel's visions and dreams, but none stands out more than the first prospect; the wheels and the creatures entwined in his opening vision. These visions hold deep meanings, which when analyzed and understood, can provide immense spiritual significance to contemporary readers.

To decode his visions we must first look at them textually, before delving into their significance. His vision of a storm coming from the north, four creatures, wheels within wheels, and an expanse over the creatures with a throne above on which sat a figure, is indeed a complex symbolism that needs discerning. Here, it is significant to note that the core of this message manifests itself as doom, transformation, and most importantly hope. It is also key to remember that these messages from Ezekiel are not delivered thematically, but symbolically. The wheels within wheels that Ezekiel saw were active, mobile, and full of eyes, symbolizing divine omnipresence and omniscience. Just like those wheels, our faith should never be passive. Even through tumultuous times, our conviction should remain active, constantly seeking wisdom and the will of God.

The creatures had four faces, symbolizing unity in diversity - embodying characteristics of wisdom (the human face), sovereignty (the lion), service (the ox), and endurance (the eagle). Similarly, one does not have to be a scholar or a mystic to decode the cryptic language of the divine. It requires one to approach the word of God with wisdom and humility while leveraging the spirit of service and persistence. The storm from the north represented doom. But within the storm, the creatures moved with the wheels upon the earth. Through this vision, Ezekiel reiterates that our God still governs in the midst of storms. This motif runs throughout the book of Ezekiel, encouraging the faithful that God is still carrying out His plans, and is in control in the storms of life.

Ezekiel's vision transcends the doom and points towards redemption. The divine figure above the expanse is a strong assertion of God's sovereignty in the face of impending destruction. Despite the loss and suffering that might have dominated their immediate reality, Ezekiel's people were reminded of their ultimate dependence on God's mercy. In decoding these visions, it is important to understand that Ezekiel's visions hold relevance to our current disposition. The wheel's movement serves as a reminder to remain steadfast in faith no matter what life throws at us. The creatures show the unity in diversity, presenting us with the insight to embrace differences, to welcome all seekers of the divine, and to live harmoniously. The storm from the north stands as a metaphor for times of hardship and tribulations where remembering God is the anchor for stability. Finally, the Divine Figure is a soothing reminder of God's eternal presence, providing hope and the much-needed resilience to face life's challenges.

The echoes of hope that reverberate from Ezekiel's visions are reminders that no level of tribulation is insurmountable, and no storm is greater than the God who calms it. Thus, in decoding Ezekiel, we gain not only a clearer understanding of its historical and cultural importance but also an introspective examination of our own faith and resilience in the face of adversity.

Verse Reference	Ezekiel's Actions	Symbolic Significance
5:1-4	Ezekiel shaves his hair and beard	Symbolizes the judgment of God
6:1-7	Ezekiel prophecies against the mountains of Israel	Symbolizes the destruction of Israel's high places
8:1-14	Ezekiel's vision of idolatry in the temple	Symbolizes God's abandonment of Jerusalem
12:1-16	Ezekiel enacts the exile of Jerusalem	Symbolizes the upcoming Babylonian captivity
24:15-24	Ezekiel's wife dies	Symbolizes the desolation of the temple
33:1-9	Ezekiel is appointed as a watchman	Symbolizes the responsibilities of prophets

In the later stages of his life, Ezekiel continued to assert his convictions and relay his prophetic visions, remaining spiritually resolute amidst the despair of exile. He teetered neither under the weight of his mission nor under the barrage of resentment from his fellow refugees. This substantial resilience is testament to the profound lessons he offered through his prophetic work:

- Ezekiel embraced his role as a watchman: Following God's appointment, Ezekiel begrudgingly accepted his position as a watchman of Israel, tasked with cautioning the people against their transgressions. The sustainability of his resilience can be attributed to this acceptance of his role and the resultant alignment of this with his actions.

- Ezekiel's honesty fortified his spiritual strength: In his work, Ezekiel never shied away from conveying difficult and hard truths as deemed necessary for his mission. This brutal honesty, though uncomfortable for the exiles and himself, bolstered his spiritual resilience.
- Ezekiel practiced unwavering obedience to God: A key component to maintaining spiritual resilience, as shown by Ezekiel, is steadfast obedience to God's directions. Despite the emotional toll his work often incited, Ezekiel's resilience found its anchor in His unswerving obedience to God, birthing the audacity to propound potentially divisive revelations.
- Ezekiel found hope in the restoration of Israel: An avid believer in God's promise to restore Israel, Ezekiel relayed visions of dry bones receiving life, a metaphor for the promised restoration. This hope served as an energizing force, enabling him to continue his watchman duties with fortitude despite the doldrums of exile.
- Ezekiel remained receptive to God's presence: Throughout isolating circumstances, Ezekiel retained his spiritual resilience by staying open to God's instructions. He was empowered by his unique encounters with God's spirit, sustaining his ability to intercede for the Israelites faithfully.

Like a heartbeat beneath a chest's cage, each lesson from Ezekiel's life thrums with resounding truth, creating a rhythm we can now internalize. Imagine the strength we might gather from embracing our spiritual roles, from practicing an uncompromising honest with ourselves, from being unwavering in obedience to God's word, from buoying faith in His promises and from staying open to His omnipresence. These lessons outline the road to spiritual resilience, acknowledged or not, walked down or left undiscovered. Remembering Ezekiel's lessons today, we rediscover faith, resilience and serenity; critical spiritual undercurrents that enliven our modern world as it did the prophet's then. These echoes of hope revealed through his resilient life may be the watchtower from which we keep vigil over our spiritual journey, ensuring we remain resilient to the tempests of time, just as Ezekiel did.

Journal Exercise:

Reflect on the role of Ezekiel as a 'spiritual watchman'. How does his mission resonate with your life today? Write down three ways in which you can assume the role of a 'watchman' in your own spiritual journey or your community. Look into the interpretation and implications of Ezekiel's prophecies. How do their messages about accountability and resilience inform your understanding of faith and how you live it out in everyday life? Also, consider an instance where you had to embody resilience in your faith. How did the experience shape your spiritual strength?

6
Minor Prophets

6.1 Jonah: Running from God's Will

In the ancient city of Nineveh resided a people whose wickedness had reached the ears of the Lord, a people drowning under the heavy burden of things done in darkness. It is in contrast to this darkness that our story begins, as the Lord calls upon the prophet Jonah, a man of God, to heed His command. The story of Jonah is an impactful narrative about faith and disobedience, revealing the profound effects that resisting spiritual conviction can have not just on individual lives, but on a whole community and even creation itself. Jonah's flight from God's will is a testament to our often inherent tendency to flee rather than embrace the challenging and transformative power of divine instruction. Yet, the story remains imbued with an undercurrent of hope, highlighting God's boundless compassion and relentless pursuit, even in our disobedience.

Charged with a divine mission to prophesy against Nineveh's wickedness, Jonah instead chose to flee, boarding a ship to Tarsish, as far away from Nineveh as he could manage. His defiance was not without consequence, for soon after he embarked on this journey, a violent storm threatened to drown the ship and the lives of those within it. Just as Jonah's spiritual disobedience was individual, so too were the consequences communal. The violent storm caused by his disobedience was not contained to just affecting him; it endangered the lives of his fellow sailors. Here we see a broader moral and spiritual lesson: Our spiritual choices and actions have ripple effects, reaching beyond our personal sphere to affect those around us in tangible ways.

As the wind roared and the sea raged, Jonah remained asleep in the lower parts of the ship, oblivious to the mayhem his disobedience had brought upon others, marking another critical insight into the nature of spiritual disobedience. Often, we may be oblivious to the chaos our actions cause, comfortably nestled in a layer of denial, while those around us bear the brunt of the storm. Subsequently, when Jonah confessed his disobedience led to the storm, the sailors threw him overboard, and the sea immediately calmed. Jonah's act of confession and the sailor's action to mitigate the situation highlights the transformative power of acknowledging our wrongdoings and taking corrective steps.

In the midst of the sea, swallowed whole by a gigantic fish, Jonah experienced the profound depths of his disobedience. In this space of isolation and reflection, he turned to God in prayer, expressing repentance and surrendering to God's will. In disobedience, Jonah experienced despair, disconnection, and distress. Yet, in his confrontation and subsequent surrender to God's will, he discovered mercy, restoration, and resurrection. This transformative journey forms a critical narrative meant to challenge, inspire, and enlighten us about faith's resilience, the wide-reaching effects of our spiritual choices, and the omnipresent hope found in God's enduring mercy and grace.

Jonah's story unveils the depths of God's merciful pursuit, demonstrating the divine orchestra of events that upends the course of our lives to accomplish the divine purpose. It presents an eloquent narration of divine providence that provokes us to reevaluate our understanding of God's intervention. From the onset, we are introduced to Jonah, a Hebrew prophet, who in his disobedience to God's instruction, boards a ship heading in the exact opposite direction of Nineveh, the city he was assigned to warn. However, this act of willful rebellion did not obliterate God's relentless pursuit.

When the sea raged, and the ship threatened to break up, the crew, driven by a divine unseen hand, chose lots to ascertain the cause of their predicament. Jonah, identified as the culprit, discloses his identity as a Hebrew and the gravity of his disobedience to the divine command. Consequently, he was thrown overboard and the sea calmed.

Verse	Theme	Interpretation
1:1-3	Jonah's Call and Flight	Jonah receives a divine mission
1:4-16	Jonah and the Storm	Jonah's disobedience creates chaos at sea.

Verse	Theme	Interpretation
1:17-2:10	The Big Fish and Jonah's Prayer	Jonah repents within the belly of a fish.
3:1-10	Jonah's Obedience and Nineveh's Repentance	Upon second call
4:1-5	Jonah's Anger and God's Reproof	Jonah expresses anger over God's mercy
4:6-11	The Lesson of the Plant	God uses a plant to teach Jonah about compassion and divine mercy.

Often, we characterize Jonah as a defiant prophet, running from God's calling. But bound in his narrative is a beautiful testament of faith's resilience and spiritual strength. Jonah's story of redemption is filled with both divine and human elements. After being swallowed by a giant fish, Jonah spent three frightening days and nights in its belly. This was neither accidental nor punitive. It was a deliberate act of divine intervention, a profound moment where Jonah, in his confinement and isolation, clung to the essence of his faith. He cried out to God in his anguish (Jonah 2:2), and in doing so, reaffirmed his trust in God.

This episode teaches us proximity to God is not necessarily about physical distance but spiritual connection. Jonah learned this the hard way. Despite finding himself in the deepest depths of the sea, he realized that he could not outrun the Lord's will, his worrisome situation instead serving as an amplifier of his spiritual dependence on God. Jonah's repentance was another display of faith's resilience. In his despair, he turned to the Lord, vowing, "What I have vowed I will pay." (Jonah 2:9). His repentance was sincere, showing a side of Jonah that was genuinely contrite and his plea for forgiveness was met with divine grace.

One may think that a man in fear for his life would say anything to escape that predicament. Though it is not unlikely, what sets Jonah's repentance apart is not the mere utterance of his repentance, but the action that followed it. After being spat out of the fish, Jonah delivered the message to Nineveh, a deed showcasing his acceptance of God's will.

Another insight from Jonah's story had to do with his faith renewal. After facing such a profound life-altering experience, Jonah was left with a renewed sense of faith and purpose. He carried out his duty, delivering the prophecy to Nineveh and witnessed the changing of hearts of an entire city. Jonah's obedience post his initial disobedience is noteworthy and shows his growth. Having strayed from God's path and suffered the consequences, he chose, in his renewed faith, to follow through on his divine mission, a testament to the strength of his belief in the Lord. But also a testimony to God's grace and willingness to bestow second chances.

In conclusion, Jonah's story is not merely about the repercussions of trying to avoid divine assignments. It's an intimate look into a man's collision with faith, redemption, and the divine; a compelling read offering key insights on how faith can revive us during challenging times, how repentance teaches us humility and fosters reconciliation, and how grace allows us to right our wrongs, imparting spiritual strength. As we navigate our journey of faith, let's remember Jonah's story - a beacon of hope, a testament to faith's resilience, and the echoes of divine grace in the grand orchestra of life.

Journal Exercise:

Begin by writing about a time when you felt you were running away from something God was prompting you towards, similar to Jonah's initial response to God's call. What was that experience like and what emotions were awakened inside of you?

As we saw in Jonah's story, running from God's will didn't lead him to peace but rather into more challenging circumstances. Did you find a similar pattern in your own story? Or possibly a different experience? Reflect and respond.

Post these considerations, express how you would respond now to the promptings of God. Have your past experiences changed your perspective towards God's will?

Finally, write a prayer where you ask God for the courage and discernibility to align with His will, no matter how challenging it may seem at first.

Remember, there are no right or wrong answers here. This is simply time for personal reflection and spiritual growth.

6.2 Amos: Social Justice and Faith

Introducing Amos, we first traverse the ancient terrains of Israel around the 8th century BC, a time marked by notable prosperity yet marred by sharp social inequities. Often regarded as the first of the classical prophets, Amos was not of royal lineage or priestly caste. His roots were that of a humble shepherd and a tender of sycamore fruit trees in Tekoa. This seemingly ordinary background played an essential role in Amos' journey, shaping his unique perspective and fueling his passion for societal fairness and justice. Drawing attention to Amos's calling, it was not a result of lineage or choice. He was not born into a prophet's family, nor did he attend a school of prophets. Rather, divinity intervened in his humble life, sending him on an ordained mission, a mission that would imprint on ages to come. Starting from tending sheep and trees, Amos found himself delivering serious messages of social justice and spiritual accountability to people far from his home, in the affluent Northern Kingdom.

Turning our gaze to the societal landscape around Amos, we find conditions that make his pursuit for justice all the more compelling. Israel was experiencing a period of peace and prosperity then. Trade flourished, wealth increased and urbanization marked the lands. However, beneath this veneer of progress and affluence, fault lines ran deep. The riches of the kingdom were concentrated in the hands of a select few, while the masses grappled with poverty. The judicial system, supposedly a refuge for the oppressed, was manipulated by the wealthy to further suppress the poor. In such a setting, Amos emerged as an ardent advocate of social justice. His messages, preserved in the biblical Book of Amos, manifested a burning zeal for righteousness, a voice for the silenced poor. He condemned practices that widened the gap between the rich and the poor, highlighted corruption in places of power, and warned of divine consequences if society failed to uphold justice.

In decoding Amos' pursuit of justice within its historical context, it is vital to analyze the powerful imagery and symbols used in his oracles. Consider the plumb line imagery in Amos 7:7-8, where God holds a plumb line, measuring the morality of the society against it. This powerful symbol, equivalent to a modern-day level used by builders, paints a vivid portrayal of how society failed to measure up to God's standards of justice and equity. It underscores the importance of ensuring that societal structures are erected on the strong foundation of social justice and moral responsibility. Analyzing the specifics, we also stumble upon the riveting paradox that underlines

Amos' messages. He was a shepherd and a fruit tender from Judah, yet his prophetic mission was primarily targeted at the northern kingdom of Israel, making him a significant outsider. This presents a poignant metaphor- an "outside" perspective is sometimes necessary to reveal the deep-seated inequities in a system.

In conclusion, understanding Amos' life in its historical context not only offers us deeper insights into his relentless pursuit for social justice, but it also reverberates far beyond his time. His advocacy for righteousness, social justice, and moral integrity are enduring principles that hold remarkable relevance in today's world. Through this lens, we observe not only the story of a humble shepherd turned prophet but a timeless advocacy for justice that resonates through the corridors of history into our lives today.

Section	Main Points	References
Introduction to Amos	Understanding the prophet's life and context	Amos 1:1
Nature of Social Injustice	Elucidating the societal issues of the time	Amos 2:6-8
Amos' Prophecies	Insight into specific predictions made	Amos 3:7
Divine Judgment	Discussion on themes of judgment in the book	Amos 5:24
Call to Repentance and Faith	Highlighting the need for repentance and trust in God	Amos 5:14-15
Conclusion on Amos	Summarizing key messages and impact	Amos 9:11-15

Centuries have passed since the shepherd of Tekoa, Amos, received his prophetic visions; their echoes, however, continue to resound, offering a blueprint for a faith-based advocacy. Investigating these often cryptic, esoteric visions offers an opportunity to reflect on the symbolism in these narratives, how they were utilized and what it means for individuals seeking a modern sense of serenity and spiritual strength. Foremost in the prophetic visions of Amos are the non-traditional symbols he employs. At a superficial level, a basket of fruit, a plumb line, and devouring locusts might appear random, if not excessively dramatic. However, Amos uses these to represent underlying messages of impending judgment, promise of restoration, and a call for justice.

Consider the vision of ripened fruit in Amos 8. While a casual onlooker may simply see a summer harvest, this symbol evokes a stark warning. Its ripeness signified Israel's maturity in sinfulness, suggesting the fullness of time - God's judgment was imminent. In modern terms, this symbolizes the necessity for recognition and resolution of personal failings.

Ostensibly more abstract, the plumb line vision in Amos 7 stands as a divine building tool symbolizing the absolute moral standard that God sets for His people. This serves as a reminder to us that faith-based advocacy should uphold the divine moral standard, promoting absolute justice, love, and mercy, principles embedded in even the most challenging Bible stories.

Equally powerful are the crops devoured by locusts in Amos 7. Here, the prophet uses imagery that would have been familiar to his agrarian audience. Today, these creeping, seemingly insignificant pests clearly illustrate the destructive potential of compounded sin – a warning for the faithful against the dangers of gradual, virtually unnoticed moral decay. Following the interpretation of these symbols, one must consider their implications for faith-based advocacy. Their basic messages are remarkably consistent and relevant: vigilance against complacency, the necessity of individual and collective moral accountability, and the embodiment of compassion and fairness.

In a quietly powerful sense, these visions underscore the importance of honest self-examination, revealing the need for constant evaluation of our actions and spiritual qualities. This mirrors the process of reading and understanding Bible stories, where thorough examination of narrative layers leads to deeper understanding, serenity, and spiritual strength. Through the symbolism laden visions, Amos powerfully critiques societal sins, notably economic exploitation and corruption. The challenge is for followers of faith to help society grapple with these issues, leveraging their influence to promote justice and equity. Beyond critique, the echoes of Amos also reveal the resilience and commitment of God's faithfulness through the promised restoration despite doom-laden visions. This in essence, is a call for sustaining hope even amidst adversity, a message that resonates with faithful suffering individual challenges today.

On a broader level, the lessons extracted from this ancient prophet point to a divine demand for the promotion of justice, love, and compassion in faith-based advocacy. This requires an unwavering commitment to fight against societal and personal sins while fostering stability and peace. The process of interpreting these ancient symbols imparts crucial wisdom for today - that the path to serenity and spiritual strength is one of continuous introspection, a sincere commitment to justice, and relentless faith in God's promises. Like the resonance of an echo, the messages within Amos' prophetic visions continue to reverberate, challenging and inspiring followers of faith to be advocates for God's transcendent values.

As we approach the modern challenges that often seem insurmountable, it's vital to look back at the principles laid out by prophet Amos. His essential teachings offer insight for cultivating resilient faith in these tumultuous times. Here's how you can apply his teachings:

Starting with empathy, an element undeniably crucial in Amos's teachings. Today's contentious social climate requires us to exercise this frequently overlooked virtue without boundary. In disagreements or misunderstandings, even when it seems impossible, step into your opponent's shoes. This simple act can break down walls, open minds, and birth essential dialogue—the cornerstone of any resolution, just as Amos advocated in his time.

Second, it is important to understand the potency of righteous indignation as taught by Amos. He demonstrated courage standing up to powerful societal institutions perpetuating social injustices. Today, it has become our responsibility to emulate such bravery. Raise your voice against any form of injustice you witness, ensuring that your indignation is driven by righteousness, not personal vendetta.

Thirdly, Amos's teachings draw attention to pressing issues of economic injustices. His prophetic vision chastised those who hoarded wealth at the expense of the poor. In our contemporary society, wealth gaps are growing and economic inequality is all too visible. It falls to us to campaign for a fairer system, wherein everyone has access to the same opportunities, financial security, and quality of life.

Next, silence in the face of sin, according to Amos is akin to complicity. We live in an era where the voices of the oppressed or marginalized often go unheard. Remaining silent in these instances aligns us with oppressors.

Instead, wherever possible, we should use our platforms to shine the light on these injustices, remaining true to the spirit of Amos.

Lastly, maintaining faith in adversity is a recurrent theme in Amos's teachings. You might feel overwhelmed by the magnitude of social crisis in the world today, but remember that faith can be your anchor. Ground yourself in the knowledge that every step taken towards justice, no matter how small, contributes to a collective movement for change.

In conclusion, the teachings of Amos offer a pathway for those wishing to navigate the often-troubled waters of modern society, seeking to make a difference. By adopting his principles of empathy, righteousness, economic justice, vocal advocacy, and unwavering faith, we can indeed build resilience and bring us closer to the peace and spiritual strength that we are destined to attain. Each day represents an opportunity, a fresh canvas on which to practice these teachings, and therein, see that hope always echoes—to the distant corners of our individual lives, and the collective conscience of modern society.

Journal Exercise:

Reflect upon the path of Amos, a shepherd turned prophet in the light of social justice and faith.

1. Write down three key insights you gained from the life and teachings of Amos. How do they resonate with your understanding of social justice and faith?
2. Amos championed the cause of the poor and challenged the complacency of the wealthy. What similar scenarios exist in our society today? In what ways can you use your faith to address these?
3. How has your understanding of faith's resilience evolved after studying this chapter?
4. Consider a circumstance in your life or in the society where you could apply the teachings of Amos. How would it modify the situation?
5. Draw a parallel between Amos's calling and your personal life. How do you feel God is calling you to act justly in your community?

Remember, there are no right or wrong answers. This is a space for you to explore your thoughts and deepen your understanding of faith and social justice.

6.3 Hosea: Love and Betrayal

Like a poignant symphony that stirs the soul, the narrative of Hosea resonates with many who have experienced heartache and forgiveness. Hosea's tale is caught between the tension of a divine love, which is boundless and unfettered, and the fallibility of human nature that often wanders astray, often heralded as betrayal. Hosea, a prophet during the 8th century BC, was commanded by God to marry a woman of ill-repute, Gomer. It initially seemed as an offense to logic and propriety. After all, why would a prophet, a sanctified man of God, connect with a woman whose flame of purity has long been extinguished? Yet, God's reasoning unveiled itself as time unrolled. Gomer's indiscretions stood as a vivid mirror reflecting Israel's spiritual adultery against God. By uniting Hosea and Gomer, God intended to protrude a strong and compelling message about His unending love for His people—despite their betrayal.

As the story unwinds itself, Gomer repeatedly returns to old patterns, involving herself in many relationships, each time breaking Hosea's heart. Hosea's response, however, is a brilliant testament to God's forgiving and redemptive love. In spite of his agony and humiliation, Hosea forgives and brings Gomer back each time. This echoes God's immense love for His erring people - profound, unwavering, and immune to human betrayal. From a modern perspective, Hosea's experiences parallel the life of the spiritually drifting individual. We sometimes find ourselves swayed away from the heavenly path by earthly distractions. Gomer's betrayal signifies our lapses of faith, her multiple infidelities mirroring our moments of doubt and digressions. Yet, each time we long for redemption, we are, like Gomer, warmly embraced and welcomed back.

In essence, Hosea's journey captures the quintessential human struggle between faith and betrayal. When we dissect this story, we are left with many significant insights:

- Hosea's divine commitment symbolizes our love for God and dedication to His word. Despite distractions, we must persevere in embracing faith.
- Gomer's repeated betrayals is a metaphor for our shortcomings. Nevertheless, these should not de-motivate or discourage us in our spiritual pursuits.

- Hosea's act of forgiving, rescuing, and restoring Gomer foreshadows God's desire for our salvation. This reaffirms that God's love is ceaseless and resilient, surpassing our imaginations.

Thus, Hosea's journey into divine love and human betrayal serves as a testament to faith's resilience. It shows that despite our betrayal, God's unconditional love never fades and His arms are ever open for our return. The echoes of hope from this tale are clear – no matter how much you fall, you can rise again, wipe clean your slate, and bask in the redeeming, warming, and loving light of God. This enduring lesson can strengthen our resolve and encourage us to persevere in our spiritual journey. In the darkest chapters of life, moments when treachery stabs the heart like a relentless dagger, few biblical figures exemplify resilience of faith more potently than Hosea, the Old Testament prophet. Hosea's story dramatically unfurls with a command from God that seems at once cruel and incomprehensible - he is ordered to marry Gomer, a woman of ill-repute, and to love her despite her constant actions of infidelity. The marriage, as foreseen, is marred with betrayal and unfaithfulness but, nonetheless, Hosea bears the painful weight.

As we traverse deeper into Hosea's life, we discover a profound truth - this story of love, betrayal, and resilience, isn't simply about Hosea and Gomer, but is a striking metaphor that mirrors the distraught relationship between God and His wayward people. God, like Hosea, loves an unfaithful partner, the children of Israel, who continually stray into the tempting allure of false idols and abandoning the one true God. The resilient faith here shown by Hosea, under God's directive, portrays a love so grotesquely divine and emboldened by the shackles of emotional pain and desolation. Over time, Hosea becomes a beacon of enduring love, unwavering faith, and existential resilience in the tempestuous sea of life's direst betrayals.

Emulating Hosea's forgiveness, we too can learn to withstand the torment of betrayal, not with resentment but with unfailing faith and love. As we navigate our divergent scriptures and lives, we can unearth these lessons:

- Love Unconditionally: Hosea loved Gomer despite her repeated betrayals. His enduring love mirrors God's infinite love for us, regardless of our unfaithfulness or wrongdoings. This stretches our understanding of resilience, emphasizing the importance of love, patience, and forgiveness in a world often overwhelmed by disappointment and bitterness.

- ❖ Learn to Forgive: One of the most staggering aspects of Hosea's narrative is the expression of forgiveness. Even after numerous infidelities, Hosea is commanded by God to accept back his wife, a remark on the boundless forgiveness of God Himself. To forgive, despite the depth of the wound, fortifies our spiritual resilience and guides us onto a path of healing and wholesomeness.
- ❖ Hope, despite Hopelessness: We find in Hosea's life an undying strand of hope. Despite the seemingly despairing situation, Hosea never relinquishes belief in the possibility of Gomer's transformation. This ardent hope is an instrumental piece of our spiritual arsenal, reminding us never to surrender to hopelessness, reinforcing our faith's resilience even in the face of stark adversity.

Through the lens of Hosea's life, we obtain a profound insight into the heart of God - endlessly patient, supremely forgiving, and boundlessly loving. In contrast to the frailties of human relationships, God's covenantal love reverberates with an exceptional quality of relentless pursuit, a searing flame that refuses to be extinguished by the chilling winds of betrayal or infidelity. As such, the echoes of Hosea's story of betrayal-to-restoration reframes our comprehension of faith's resilience, underpinning the essence of divine forgiveness and transformative love. It beseeches us to emulate this resilience in our personal journeys, calling us ever onward, toward a hope that endures, a faith that thrives, and a love that never ceases.

With the understanding gained about Hosea's exemplary acts of love and forgiveness, we can hasten to apply these lessons in our own lives, to achieve modern serenity and enhance spiritual strength. This spiritual strength can be the propelling force that instigates change not only within individual hearts but also within the communities we inhabit. Drawing from the wealth of Hosea's deep-seated lessons, we can adapt some crucial strategies for maintaining tranquility in our current era and enriching our spiritual resilience:

1. Embracing Unconditional Love: Hosea's willingness to redeem Gomer, despite her actions, depicted an embodiment of unconditional love. Drawing from his resilience, we can learn to love people not for what they can offer us or how they treat us, which can waver, but for who they are - irreplaceable, worthy human beings. This form of agape love fosters inner peace and satisfaction.
2. Forgive Persistently: Learning from Hosea's character, unrelenting forgiveness should be part of our relational dynamics. Our choice to

forgive does not condone the actions of the wrongdoer but liberates our hearts from the heavy shackles of hurt. This fortifies our mind in the face of adversity and augments our spiritual strength.

3. Hope and Faith as a Bedrock: Despite the seemingly insurmountable challenges Hosea faced, his unswerving faith and hope in God never wavered. Like Hosea, clinging to hope and faith, particularly during our most trying moments, can be our stable bedrock. This cultivates a serene state of mind capable of withstanding the nightmares of modern life.
4. Reconciliation and Redemption: Reconciliation with and redemption of oneself are other essential aspects we can glean from Hosea's narrative. Recognizing our personal faults and consciously making efforts to mend our ways achieves self-redemption. This wholehearted acceptance and willingness to change induces a sense of calmness and enhances spiritual growth.

In adopting these practical strategies reaped from Hosea's story into our lives, we position ourselves to navigate the tumultuous waves of modernity with serenity. The beauty of these lessons lies not merely in their understanding but their application. Remember, true serenity and spiritual strength aren't attained by a one-off event; they are the product of a continuous, consistent, dedicated practice. Hosea's story stands as a comforting reminder that we, too, possess the resilience to face life's unexpected challenges with grace. Indeed, the gems gleaned from his undying love and forgiveness are within our reach to claim; it lies in the echo of hope that resonates within us all. Lean into this hope, let it shape the narrative of your life and watch as you grow resilient in faith, serene amidst chaos, and stronger in spirit.

Verse Number	Main Events	Characters Involved
1	Hosea's prophecy begins	Hosea
2	Hosea marries Gomer	Gomer
3	Gomer is unfaithful	Gomer
4	Children are born	Hosea
5	Gomer leaves Hosea	Gomer
6	Hosea forgives and redeems Gomer	Hosea

Journal Exercise:

1. Reflect on a time when you experienced betrayal. How did you handle the situation?
2. Compare your response to the love-filled approach Hosea took despite Gomer's betrayals. In what ways do you find his actions challenging?
3. Imagine if you were in Hosea's shoes, would you have done things differently? Why or why not?
4. Hosea's love for Gomer is a portrayal of God's unconditional love for us. In what ways have you experienced such love in your own life?
5. Finally, write a prayer to God focusing on forgiveness, love, and resilience in the face of betrayal. Ask for strength to love as selflessly as Hosea loved Gomer even in difficult times.

7
The Life and Teachings of Jesus

7.1 The Beatitudes: A Manifesto for Spiritual Resilience

As we delve beneath the surface, the brilliant brilliance of the Beatitudes stands out as a lighthouse guiding us through life's turbulent waves. This mesmerizing portion of the Sermon on the Mount, found in Matthew 5:3-12, does more than prescribe moral virtues, it conveys a deep-seated blueprint for spiritual resilience, crafting an epic saga of blessedness interlaced with spiritual survival.

"Blessed are the poor in spirit, for theirs is the kingdom of heaven," announces Jesus commencing the Beatitudes. Here, 'poor in spirit' connects to a state of spiritual humility, recognizing our deep need for divine intervention. This humble acknowledgement of spiritual poverty forms the cornerstone of spiritual resilience, a disciplined to and fro movement between reliance on divine grace and human effort. Those who truly understand their vulnerability, strength, and purpose within this dynamic are characterized as 'blessed', and theirs undeniably, is the assurance of heavenly reward.

It's intriguing to note the reciprocity infused in each Beatitude, acting as spiritual sustenance during periods of desolation or uncertainty. For instance, "Blessed are they who mourn, for they shall be comforted" portrays a profound consolation in times of distress. The language employed subtly reassures us that sorrow is not an absolute state; hope is always within grasp, personified as comfort extended to those who mourn. Each tear sowed germinates as a seed of comfort, a testament to the resilience of faith. Further, the Beatitudes invite us on a journey of self-reflection, promoting peace-making, meekness, and a thirst for righteousness as gateways to blessedness. The journey, however, is not without trials and tribulation.

"Blessed are you when people insult you, persecute you and falsely say all kinds of evil against you because of me," proclaims the final Beatitude. Here, persecution is intricately connected with faith's resilience. When opposition against faith emerges, and conventions defy morale, the choice to maintain spiritual fortitude demonstrates resilience.

In this context, persecution becomes an instrument of spiritual strengthening rather than a deterrent. The blessedness associated with such persecution speaks volumes about the resilience born of faith, validating the phrase, 'what doesn't kill you, makes you stronger'. Moreover, the promise of a great reward in heaven serves as a beacon of hope, echoing the ultimate victory of faith over adversity. Overall, the Beatitudes beautifully marry the concept of blessedness with spiritual survival, unlocking the vast realms of spiritual resilience. Such resilience is not accessed through a mundane rigidity or obstinacy against life's vicissitudes, but through an embrace that transcends temporal discomfort with a view set firmly on the heavenly reward. Such is the potency of blessedness as defined by the Beatitudes, reinforcing the resilience of faith to withstand, endure, and indeed, to thrive amidst adversities. To grasp the profound wisdom embedded in the beatitudes, it's crucial first to understand what they embody: a heartfelt expression of faith amidst trials. Each beatitude tells a story of resilience, of individuals who have faced oppressive adversities and yet found solace in their divine faith.

Beginning with the first Beatitude, "Blessed are the poor in spirit, for theirs is the kingdom of heaven" (Matthew 5:3). This verse invites us to humility and dependence on God, recognizing our need for Him in every moment of life. It's a constant reminder to surrender our pride and to place our trust in the Lord, especially when encountering challenges.

Next comes the second Beatitude, "Blessed are they who mourn, for they shall be comforted" (Matthew 5:4). This passage extends reassurance to those grappling with pain and loss. As you traverse through the hardships of life, it reminds you that the Lord is your comforter, next to you amidst your trials. He is the ultimate source of consolation that heals both visible and hidden wounds.

"Blessed are the meek, for they shall inherit the earth" (Matthew 5:5). It's a potent reminder of the power of humility and gentleness, virtues often overlooked in our fast-paced, assertive society. This verse urges us to uphold our values, even amidst struggles, knowing that ultimate reward awaits.

Likewise, each proceeding Beatitude reveals the underlying resilience of faith amidst trials. As you venture into the complexities of life, it's essential to remember these precious lessons of hope, strength, and wisdom from the beatitudes. They serve as remarkable anchors and resources, enabling you to maintain your faith and resilience amidst all kinds of pressures. Reflected in these verses are the divine truths of faith's resonance: the promise of spiritual riches for the humble, comfort for the mourning, and abundance for the meek. The Beatitudes continue to resonate with timeless, universal relevance, infusing a renewed sense of strength and resilience within modern believers.

These practical lessons drawn from the Beatitudes can be incorporated into our daily life:

- Embracing humility: Recognize the strength in vulnerability and the grace powerful enough to meet us at our lowliest — it's in these moments that we learn to truly depend on God.
- Comfort in mourning: Understanding that our sorrow is seen, is known, and is met with divine comfort can nourish our resilience during challenging times.
- Upholding meekness: It may seem contrary to the world's portrayal of strength, but these verses remind us of the eventual honor reserved for the gentle and humble.

Continue to reflect on these lessons, replicate them in your daily life, and keep lighting the silent whispers of faith and resilience amidst your trials. The Beatitudes are reminders of hope; their echoes resonate with the heartbeat of divine comfort and reassurance. They hold a bifocal lens, encouraging us to remain steadfast through hardships while focusing on the promise of an eternal reward. So, in times of adversity, remember to anchor yourself in these beats of hope and let your faith bloom, even amidst the direst of trials.

One of the most prominent sections in the Holy Scripture, which directly deals with achieving serenity and peace, is known as the Beatitudes. These are the teachings of Jesus from the Sermon on the Mount, where he speaks of blessings and virtues which uphold spiritual strength and resilience. Each Beatitude begins with 'Blessed are they...' and presents a clear pathway to internal harmony and tranquility. Even though they were taught centuries ago, their profound wisdom continues to provide valuable lessons for our modern lives. Let's decipher the Beatitudes and understand how they can guide us in maintaining spiritual resilience in our day-to-day existence.

1. "Blessed are the poor in spirit, for theirs is the kingdom of heaven." This Beatitude teaches us the value of humility and the importance of accepting our own spiritual impoverishment. In acknowledging our inherent need for God, we find the first steps towards inner peace. By fully surrendering to God's will, and not relying solely on our own abilities, we uncover the deep reservoir of divine peace that surpasses all understanding.
2. "Blessed are they who mourn, for they shall be comforted." Grief, in its own way, brings us closer to the understanding of the impermanence of worldly possession and relationships. It helps us behold the promise of God's eternal comfort. Thus, mourning is not a sign of lack of spiritual strength but rather a part of human existence leading us towards long-lasting peace.
3. "Blessed are the meek, for they shall inherit the earth." True strength, after all, does not lie in our ability to control others or in domineering attitudes. The strength of the spirit lives in our capacity for kindness, consideration and patience - it lies in the essence of humility.
4. "Blessed are they who hunger and thirst for righteousness, for they shall be satisfied." A desire for justice, for righteousness, is what can lead us towards a state of internal calm. As we strive for fairness in all our dealings, we pave the way for spiritual serenity.
5. "Blessed are the merciful, for they shall obtain mercy." Mercy is not just about forgiving others, it's about cultivating a forgiving and compassionate attitude towards oneself. It's the seed of inner peace.
6. "Blessed are the pure in heart, for they shall see God." A heart that is free from duplicity and malice is capable of knowing God on a deeper level - thus experiencing a profound sense of peace.
7. "Blessed are the peacemakers, for they shall be called the children of God." Seeking to establish peace with others and staying away from conflicts is not only a vital characteristic of a child of God but a means to maintain our inner calm.
8. "Blessed are those who are persecuted for righteousness' sake, for theirs is the kingdom heaven." Lastly, the willingness to stand by what is good, even in the face of adversity, displays spiritual resilience. This surrendering and steadfastness in righteousness carries a promise of eternal peace.

By integrating these teachings into our daily life, we can achieve a state of serenity and tranquility. The Beatitudes are rudimentary yet profound instructions that can assist in forging an unbroken connection between our faith and daily struggles. In them, we find comfort, guidance, and the echoing resilient hope which can help us maintain spiritual strength in our modern hectic life.

Beatitude Number	Text	Relevance
1	Blessed are the poor in spirit	Recognizes humility
2	Blessed are those who mourn	Encourages emotional honesty
3	Blessed are the meek	Suggests value in gentleness
4	Blessed are those who hunger and thirst for righteousness	Affirms relentless pursuit of justice
5	Blessed are the merciful	Advocates for compassion and forgiveness
6	Blessed are the pure in heart	Promotes sincerity and authenticity

Journal Exercise:

1. After reading Matthew 5:3-10, identify one Beatitude that resonates with you the most. Write about a personal situation where you can apply it.
2. Write about your interpretations of the Beatitude, how it impacts your life, and what changes you wish to make to embody this Beatitude fully.
3. Reflect upon how Jesus' teachings on the Beatitudes challenge the world's values. How do they offer a kind of spiritual resilience that the world can't? Express your thoughts on this.
4. The Beatitudes are promises of blessings. Which of these blessings do you desire the most and why?
5. Imagine Jesus personally speaking the Beatitudes to you. How does each Beatitude speak to your present condition? Record your insights.

Remember, there is no right or wrong answer – let your spirit lead you in this reflective exercise.

7.2 Parables: Revealing the Kingdom of God

Bible parables beautifully encapsulate the essence of faith's fortitude and resilience. They are ingrained with a deep wisdom that offers us guidance, peace, and strength. The scriptures are often like a treasure chest, with layers of meaning just waiting to be unveiled, interpreted, and understood. These stories serve as metaphoric representations of life's greatest trials, tribulations, rewards, and virtues. Let's unpack some of these parabolic narratives, peeling back the layers and deciphering what truly lies beneath. Herein lies the art of metaphor: uncovering the hidden symbolism embedded within.

- The Parable of the Mustard Seed: An insignificantly small seed that grows into one of the largest trees. Here, Jesus is speaking about faith - a comparison to the mustard seed. Our faith, albeit small in the beginning, has the capacity to grow and blossom into something immensely powerful and unshakeable.
- The Parable of the Prodigal Son: A story of a young man who squanders his fortune, lives a life of destitution, and returns home to face a forgiving father. This parable is a testament to God's infinite love and mercy, indicating that no matter how far we may slip away, His love is unwavering. It speaks to the resilience of faith.
- The Parable of the Lost Coin: This tale of a woman who, upon losing one of her ten coins, diligently sweeps her house until she uncovers it, invites us to understand God's relentless search for lost souls. It serves as a timeless reminder that every life matters to God.

The parables are tools of spiritual empowerment, meant to stir faith, foster resilience, and offer solace. These rich narratives are more than just entertaining tales; they are vibrant life-lessons dressed in metaphor. Like any art form, they require patience, observation, and contemplation to grasp their profound essence. Now, as we step into deciphering these metaphors, remember to approach them with an open heart and farsighted vision. What you find may not only surprise you but also equip you with a newfound strength and unshakeable faith.

Parable Name	Message	Scriptural Reference
Sower	The response to the Word of God varies according to the state of one's heart	Matthew 13:3-9
Weeds amongst Wheat	The kingdom of God would be corrupted by evil	but in the end
Mustard Seed	Even though the kingdom of God may start small	it will grow exponentially and provide shelter for many
Leaven	The kingdom of God will pervade and transform the whole world	Matthew 13:33
Hidden Treasure	The kingdom of God is of such great value that one should be willing to give up everything else for it	Matthew 13:44
Pearl of Great Price	The kingdom of God is worth seeking and sacrificing all to possess	Matthew 13:45-46

Stepping forward into the world of parables, the stories with deep inherent meanings folded into the narrative, we find individuals acting as personifications of faith. Here we seek to understand who these individuals are, the stories they live through, and the lessons they provide.

Consider the story of the Prodigal Son in Luke 15:11-32, a tale unfolding in a non-judgmental environment opening the doors for the protagonist to learn and grow. This young man embodies a form of faith that stumbles, falls, yet finds the will to rise again and go back home to the Father. His faith may not have been perfect, never wavering, yet it was real and resilient. When faced with hardships borne from his own actions, he confesses and repents, demonstrating a faith that is lived and experienced rather than merely spoken. Opposite to him stands his older brother, a character that surfaces the subtle facets of faith. His faith is convicting but also reveals an undertone of self-righteousness, jealousy, and lack of compassion. This brother's faith is a stark reminder that faith must resonate with love and sincerity, and not be a mere obligation or expectation of reward.

The Good Samaritan in Luke 10:25-37 allows us another angle of viewing faith's nature. Carrying faith in one's heart is more than following religious laws and principles; it's about embodying God's love. The Samaritan, though he was considered an outsider and enemy by Jewish laws, displays great compassion and love, exemplifying faith in action. His selfless act challenges us to embody faith in our actions, making us active participants in the compassionate love that scripture teaches us. In contrast, take a glance at the Parable of the Talents in Matthew 25:14-30. Each servant is granted talents, and their actions afterward provide insights into different degrees and understandings of faith. The servant who hides his talent out of fear showcases a faith rooted in fear and misunderstanding of God's nature. The servants who use their talents well paint an optimism, emphasizing the gain through faith rooted in understanding and trust.

And who could overlook the Parable of the Sower in Matthew 13:1-23? The seed sown on various grounds representing men's hearts teaches us how faith can vary; faith that is too shallow, distracted by worldly worries or enabling of sin fails to yield fruit. However, faith that is deeply rooted within us is resilient, resists temptation, and brings forth good fruits.

These protagonists invite us to introspect. Do we hold faith out of fear, like the servant who hid the talent, or do we move towards compassionate love like the Good Samaritan? At times, we may find ourselves like the Prodigal Son, torn and brought back by faith's resilience, or perhaps we resonate with the sown seed on various grounds, experiencing different degrees and implications of faith. To delve deep into faith's resilience, one must not shy away from asking which character they recognize in themselves. In recognizing our reflections within these parables and accepting our strengths and failings, we embark on a journey that directs us towards a deeper, more profound faith, typing the bond between ancient scripture and our modern serenity and strength. These personifications of faith serve as reminders, teaching aids, and mirrors, guiding our steps on the path of spiritual growth. Embrace reflection, embrace growth, and above all, embrace faith.

The parables in the Bible stood the test of time - their wisdom transcends generations to offer relevant insights to modern minds. By delving into them and their spiritual depths, we can commence our transfer from knowledge to transformation. Let us consider the powerful life lessons these biographies and narratives offer:

In the tale of Joseph, we treasure the wonder of divine orchestration. Despite repeatedly falling into harsh circumstances - sold into slavery, wrongly accused, and unfairly imprisoned - Joseph never lost sight of God's greater plan. He teaches us about unbroken trust. In our modern world, overwhelmed by hardships and insecurity, Joseph's story reminds us to remain patient and trust in divine timing. This trust can bring stability, serenity, and spiritual strength.

Lesson two emerges from the story of Moses. He was prompted to approach Pharaoh for the release of his people, a task he felt utterly unqualified for. Despite his self-doubt and fear, Moses obeyed, empowering each of us to override personal inhibitions for a cause greater than ourselves. Today, we might be the Moses needed in our community or family, around our workplace or social group, to instigate real change.

The bravery of David in the face of Goliath continues to inspire as we face what can feel like insurmountable odds. He approached the frightening giant not with traditional armory but with faith and a humble sling. His victory serves as a lesson of audacious faith in God transcending human fright and inadequacy. This fearlessness, rooted in faith, can provide modern seekers a peace that overrides worldly anxieties and doubts, stitching them into the fabric of spiritual strength.

Unpacking the supreme life of Jesus, one gleans the power of servitude from the ultimate example of servant hood in washing His disciples' feet. Despite His status, Jesus purposefully served, showcasing that true greatness stems from the position of a servant. In a world enamored with grandeur and domination, such humility and service reorient ambitions towards genuine love and compassion, cultivating tranquil hearts filled with spiritual strength.

Finally, Ruth and Naomi present love in its purest, most resilient form. In the face of loss and heartache, Ruth remained dedicated to her mother-in-law. Her devotion paved the way for Boaz's love and their lineage extending to Jesus. Her narrative underlines the power of loyalty and deep love underpinning life's vibrant tapestry, fostering serenity amid emotional torrents and spiritual fortitude within and around us.

In summary, the Bible's rich narratives unravel a plethora of wisdom. Woven through these stories is a profound understanding of resilience, faith, obedience, servitude, humility and love – elements deeply pertinent to modern living. Unearthing these messages of hope allows their echoes to resonate in day-to-day life, fostering serenity and spiritual strength in the dynamic rhythm of modern times. Thus, we can say with confidence, transferring ancient parabolic wisdom into today's context is not only possible but also life-transforming.

Journal Exercise:

Begin with writing down what you think the 'Kingdom of God' signifies based on the parables discussed in the chapter. Then, choose one of the parables that resonates most with you and briefly explain why. Reflect on how this parable might apply to your life today.

Finally, imagine you were to narrate a modern-day parable that communicates a similar message about the 'Kingdom of God'. What would your story look like in current times? Write this parable down, focusing on the elements that make it relevant and relatable for today's world.

7.3 Sermon on the Mount: The Ethics of the Kingdom

The Beatitudes, a profound sermon from Jesus found in the Gospel of Matthew, sets the foundation for understanding the essence of divinity encapsulated in humility. Through these beautifully crafted statements, Jesus not only presents a new paradigm for engaging with the divine but also paves the way for achieving modern serenity and spiritual strength. The first Beatitude, "Blessed are the poor in spirit, for theirs is the kingdom of heaven," is a resounding call for humility. In this context, being poor in spirit doesn't suggest material poverty but rather a humble acknowledgment of our spiritual insufficiency. It reminds us that, stripped of all worldly attachments and preconceptions about spirituality, we are all in need of divine grace. By adopting a stance of spiritual poverty, we position ourselves to be entirely dependent on God's mercy. This unconditional dependence unlocks the gate to heavenly riches that remain closed to the prideful. It teaches us to find serenity in the realization that, without God, we can do nothing, yet with Him, nothing is impossible.

Furthermore, Christ's second Beatitude, "Blessed are those who mourn, for they will be comforted," presents a countercultural viewpoint. Through this statement, Jesus reminds his followers that mourning is not a deteriorative state, but rather a raw and genuine experience of the human condition that opens up room for divine comfort and spiritual growth. It serves as an echo of hope for those navigating through difficulties, assuring that their tears will not go disregarded. Going deeper into this beatitude helps us realize that mourning, whether over personal wrongdoing, injustice in the world, or loss of a loved one, shouldn't be avoided. Instead, it should be embraced as an opportunity to experience divine comfort. Just as a seed must first be buried in darkness before sprouting up toward the light, spiritual growth often transpires in the fertile soil of sorrow.

The third Beatitude challenges us even further. "Blessed are the meek, for they will inherit the earth." Often misunderstood, meekness isn't synonymous with weakness; rather, it signifies strength under control. It involves yielding our power, not in passivity or resignation, but in unwavering trust in God's wisdom and sovereign will. In a world that glorifies audacious assertions of personal power, the call towards meekness is audaciously contrarian. It invites us into a peaceful coexistence, with humility as our badge of honor and love for our fellow humans as our compass. In heeding this call, we become heirs of the Earth, custodians of God's beautiful creation, living harmoniously with each other, ourselves, and our Creator.

When we start following these teachings, the echoes of hope reverberate through our lives. We begin to seek wealth in spiritual poverty, comfort in mourning, and authority through humility. By immersing ourselves in the quintessence of the Beatitudes, we not only discover a blueprint for resilient faith but also unlock the path for divine serenity and strength.

Verse	Message	Application
Matt 5:3	Blessed are the poor in spirit	Spiritual humility
Matt 5:4	Blessed are those who mourn	Comfort in loss
Matt 5:6	Blessed are those who hunger and thirst for righteousness	Pursuit of Justice
Matt 6:14	For if you forgive other people	Art of Forgiving
Matt 7:12	So in everything do to others what you would have them do to you	Golden Rule

Bearing the portrait of Kingdom ethics embodied in stories and teachings, the Lord's Prayer stands out as a stellar example. With roots in the heart of the Sermon on the Mount, it provides us not with a rigid prayer routine, but a profound reflection of discernment, wisdom, and kingdom values - values that are ever-relevant in the lives we lead today.

In further unearthing these values, let us delve into an in-depth analysis of the Lord's Prayer and its sentiments.

"Our Father in heaven,
hallowed be your name."

The opening line epitomizes the essence of recognizing the divine - the celestial being, God our Father, the architect and manner of all. The connotation of hallowed, meaning sacred or respected, showcases the unwavering reverent awe for God.

Much more, this reiterates the quintessential value of respect and sanctity: not just towards the divine, the sacred and the holy, but also towards every being, every life, and every creation in our common earthly realm.

"Your kingdom come,
your will be done,
on earth as it is in heaven."

The quest for equilibrium between the heavenly and our earthly realm reflects the constant pursuit of balance and serenity in our lives. Drawing parallels with the prayer, our lives must not only be about always seeking the heavenly perfection, or being engrossed with the earthly changes, but finding a harmonized blend where the spiritual strength fuels our pursuit of ethical living in our everyday experiences here on earth.

"Give us this day our daily bread."

This statement prompts a profound contrast against the age of excessiveness and immediate gratification that modern society often finds itself in. The prayer's plea is a reminder of the essential value of gratitude for our daily provision, against the backdrop of desires and wants.

"And forgive us our debts,
as we also have forgiven our debtors."

The prayer shifts its focus towards forgiveness, an often overlooked aspect of our dealing with self and others. We are encouraged to seek forgiveness and to forgive. This practice not only fosters peace with others but also brings peace within. The virtue of forgiveness can help us veer away from resentment and bitterness, leading to emotional tranquility and spiritual strength.

"And lead us not into temptation,
but deliver us from evil."

Resilience in faith echoes through this verse. Life's journey is ripe with challenges and moments of trials. This verse teaches resilience. It affirms surrender and trust in the divine to deliver us from adversities, echoing a profound truth: Our spiritual fortitude, the strength of our faith, will guide us through everything. Interpreting the lines of this timeless prayer, we discover the ethos of Kingdom ethics - values that not only bridge the gap between the divine and the human but also guide us towards a mindful living that is spiritually enriching and emotionally fulfilling. Each verse catapults us into a theological and practical journey, querying us, refining us, and urging us to resist, to surrender, to look beyond and within, all at once.

The Lord's Prayer is not just a set verse for ritualistic repetitions but is a template for life, a guide to practical and spiritually resilient living. This prayer reflects the ultimate aspiration of the soul: to attain inner peace, realize divine love, become a channel of blessings, and manifest the Kingdom ethics in every stride of life. Hence, may we find resilience and solace in embodying these timeless values in our everyday existence. As our journey of spiritual growth continues, it's fundamental to explore the essence of righteous living as embodied in the Sermon on the Mount, a monumental discourse given by Jesus Christ. This richly symbolic sermon isn't merely a set of directives but an avenue to spiritual fullness and tranquility that speaks volumes to contemporary society.

From "Blessed are the poor in spirit" to "Blessed are those who are persecuted", the beatitudes set the tone for what it means to live righteously. It's a call to cultivate virtues such as humility, empathy, mercy, and the pursuit of righteousness. It's not about subscribing to a list of prohibitions, instead, it's about embracing virtues that align us more closely with the divine, promoting peace within ourselves and with others.

A closer look at the beatitudes:

- The poor in spirit: This message isn't praising material poverty, but rather, spiritual humility. It's an invitation to acknowledge our imperfections and embrace our dependence on the divine.
- Those who mourn: Grieving is human, and in this, Jesus reassures us of divine comfort. It's a lesson in empathy, connoting that our sorrows and those of others are known and felt by God.
- The meek: Jesus extols the virtue of gentleness—people not domineered by ego but are humble and considerate.
- The hunger and thirst for righteousness: To desire fairness for oneself and others is praised. It carries the lesson of endurance and tenacity, persisting in the pursuit of what's morally right.

Next, we encounter the segment on the law in which Christ articulated the importance of moral righteousness. He essentially expands the precepts of the law to include the essence of the heart, advocating for sincerity and purity of intentions alongside deeds. In focusing on aspects such as Murder, Adultery, Oaths, we see a shift from adherence to the letter of the law towards a deeper, heart-centered righteousness. Murder isn't merely physically taking a life—it extends to unrighteous anger and unkind words. Similarly, adultery isn't merely unfaithfulness in marriage—it includes nurturing impure thoughts.

The teachings of the Sermon on the Mount tend towards the practice of 'love for enemies', a seemingly paradoxical commandment. It's a profound lesson in unconditional love. Righteous living is about nurturing an encompassing love that extends even towards those we perceive as enemies.

Finally, Jesus speaks of the vital need for sincerity in prayer, charitable deeds, fasting, laying up treasures in heaven, the inability to serve God and wealth, trusting in divine provision and not being judgmental. In essence, living righteously, as encapsulated in the teachings of the Sermon on the Mount, isn't about a mundane rigid code, but an inward transformation—a loving and faithful response to the divine that results in personal growth and communal harmony. By living according to these principles, we can perfect a spirituality that bestows serenity and strength in our modern lives.

Journal Exercise:

Take a few moments to reflect on the teaching given in the Sermon on the Mount. How can these teachings be applied to your daily life? Write about a specific situation where you could apply one of these teachings. What are the potential outcomes of this application, both positive and negative?

Next, consider the ethics of the kingdom as described in the chapter. How do they compare to today's societal norms and values? Write about the similarities and differences, and how as a Christian, you can ensure kingdom ethics are being practiced in your daily interactions.

Lastly, what are your thoughts about the Kingdom's ethics relevance in today's world? Do you believe they are still applicable, or need modification? Discuss why you feel this way, and what it means for you as a Christian living in the modern age.

7.4 The Crucifixion and Resurrection: Ultimate Faith and Hope

Through the pages of the Gospel, we journey alongside Jesus Christ, observing His faith, resilience, and ultimate sacrifice for all of humanity. His passage to Calvary stands as a stark reminder of His consistent faith in the divine plan and His profound love for mankind. Jesus' last days were filled with trials and tribulations, His final journey started from the isolating Garden of Gethsemane. Essences of uncertainty and despair threaded the atmosphere, yet Christ held steadfast in His faith. He beseeched God, "Father, if thou be willing, remove this cup from me: nevertheless not my will, but thane, be done." (Luke 22:42). In the face of such grueling adversity, He upheld the ultimate principle of faith - surrender to God's will. His resilience demonstrated in this moment of crisis serves as a strong reference point for modern Christians.

Journeying forward, Jesus traversed the halls of Pontius Pilate's palace. Despite the damning accusations leveled against Him, He remained serene and silent, embodying the proverb in Isaiah 53:7, "He was oppressed, and He was afflicted; yet He opened not His mouth." His silence reflected His infinite wisdom and the depth of His faith, rooted not in His words, but in His actions.

We see another example in the encounter with Simon of Cyrene. Reluctantly thrust into carrying Christ's cross, Simon found himself intertwined in one of history's most significant narratives. Here, Jesus taught Simon – and all of us - the essence of shared suffering. Regardless of our reluctance or the circumstances, when we are called to carry a burden, we are invited to join in His redemptive work on humanity's behalf. At the Cross of Calvary, his loving heart was pierced, and from it flowed water and blood, symbols of the sacraments of Baptism and the Holy Eucharist. While His body was ravaged, His faith stood unbroken. In the throes of His mortal agony, His final words were a testament to His unwavering faith, "Father, into thy hands I commend my spirit." (Luke 23:46).

Therefore, Christ's journey to Calvary is an embodiment of strong faith in the face of immense suffering. This narrative teaches us that:

- ❖ Faith does not equate to having all answers or escaping suffering. It is about trust and surrender to God.
- ❖ Our silence can speak volumes about our faith and resilience, especially during testing times.
- ❖ We all have our crosses to bear, and carrying them can become a part of God's plans for our redemption.
- ❖ In life and in death, committing ourselves to God's care reflects our ultimate faith and trust in Him.
- ❖ Faith's resilience transcends physical pain and suffering, guiding us towards spiritual strength and inner peace.

These valuable lessons remind us of the indispensable role of faith in strengthening our spiritual resilience and serenity amidst modern life's challenges. Emulating Christ's unwavering faith, we can rest in the assurance that even in our suffering, we are never forsaken but continually held in the loving embrace of God. Exploring the crucifixion, we delve into an act of self-sacrifice that serves as a testament to faith's resilience and the power that deeply rooted spiritual beliefs can hold. The story of Jesus' crucifixion presents a paradoxical model of suffering, sacrifice, and ultimately victory. As we engage with this seminal biblical narrative, we encourage you to apply the lessons and principles leaned upon your own personal journey for spiritual strength and peace.

Jesus, knowing the fate that awaited him, accepted his approaching demise with grace and dignity. This profound acceptance was not a reflection of passive resignation, but a testament to His divine understanding of the necessity of His self-sacrifice. This echoes the same resilience we can find in our modern life when faced with adversity. The ability to stand tall, in spite of looming trials, is something that requires not only strength but a resilient faith. He was betrayed, mocked, beaten, and sentenced to death on false grounds. Yet, even in the face of such trials, His spirit remained unbroken. He prayed to the Father, 'Forgive them, for they do not know what they're doing'. This offers an invaluable lesson on forgiveness and empathy. Even when faced with the harshest of situations, He maintained His benevolence. His unwavering kindness, even towards those who cause hurt, paves the way for us to practice empathy and forgiveness in our own lives.

At the same time, the Crucifixion is a testament to the power of hope and faith, even in the most desperate of situations. Jesus knew that His life ended there, but He also held faith in the plan set forth by God. His resurrection on the third day validated His faith and exemplified the power of resilience and hope. This teaches us the importance of maintaining faith and hope regardless of our present circumstances. Amidst these trials, when put on the cross, Jesus said, 'It is finished'. The seeming finality of His declaration held within it a hidden promise of a beginning. His death marked the start of a new spiritual journey for humanity, a redeeming journey that ended with His resurrection. The crucifixion wasn't the end, but a transformation. This gives us the impetus to perceive endings not as completions but as beginnings of something new, to perceive adversity as an opportunity for growth.

The Crucifixion's remembrance helps maintain the symbolic resonance it holds for Christ's followers across the globe. However, irrespective of individual beliefs, the crucifixion story offers a profound lesson on resilience in the face of adversity, mercy, forgiveness, hope, and unconditional love. It is a reminder that spiritual strength and serenity lies in our capacity to endure, to hope, and to love.

Event	Significance	Interpretation
Crucifixion	Ultimate Sacrifice	Sign of total obedience
Last Supper	New Covenant	Symbolic representation of sacrifice
Resurrection	Victory over Death	The foundation of Christian Hope

Event	Significance	Interpretation
Apostles' witness	Spread of Gospel	Solidifying the resurrection truth
Pentecost	Coming of the Holy Spirit	Empowerment of the Church
Ascension	Jesus' return to Fatherly throne	Promise of His return

In the early morning, as the women arrived at the tomb, they found it empty – an event that seemed incomprehensible to them, as they were expecting to prepare Jesus' body for a proper burial. Yet, in the vacancy of the tomb, lay an indisputable evidence of His resurrection - a foundational event that spurred the growth of Christian faith and hope. The resurrection emphasized the triumph of faith in numerous distinctive ways.

- At first, it validated the prophetic utterances of Jesus about His death and subsequent resurrection. Throughout His teachings, He regularly spoke of these events as an assurance of His divine purpose and assignment. The realization of His words and the accomplishment of this prophecy only served to fortify the faith of His followers.
- Secondly, the resurrection provided a concrete, tangible evidence of God's omnipotence, accentuating the reality of His sovereign power over even death itself. This demonstration ignited within His followers a resilient faith that God truly possesses absolute jurisdiction over all realms of existence, including the physical and the spiritual, the temporal and the eternal.
- Lastly, the resurrection signified victory over sin and its consequence - death. This triumph communicated to Jesus' followers the supreme power of faith in God's plan of redemption. The death of Jesus served as the ransom for sin, but His resurrection accentuated the conquest over sin and death, an accomplishment only possible through God's infinite power.

In addition to asserting the victory of faith, the resurrection of Jesus also marked the dawn of eternal hope. This hope was embodied in the promise Jesus made to His followers, that He was preparing a place for them in His Father's house, and that He would return to take them there. The resurrection therefore, served as a guarantee of this promise, a beacon of eternal hope that transcends earthly trials and tribulations.

- The resurrection indicates the pledge of eternal life, a life unmarred by suffering, sorrow or death. The concept of eternal life is not merely an extension of temporal existence, but a quality of life interconnected with God, filled with His perfection, love, and joy. It is this hope of eternal life that allows the spirit to endure in times of adversity and to remain firm in the face of earthly afflictions.
- Just as Christ was resurrected, so too, the resurrection promised the rebirth and transformation of the mortal bodies of believers into glorified ones, free from the burdens of sin and corruption - another boost to the believer's hope.

The resurrection story is a narrative of victory - the triumph of faith over doubt, of love over hate, of life over death. It heralds the advent of a hope that persists in the darkness, a hope that is intrinsically tied to the faith in eternal life. It reinforces the belief that Jesus is the Messiah, validating all His teachings and promises, and reaffirms that through Him, believers have access to the comfort, peace, and strength they require to explore their personal faith journey. Echoing across centuries, the resurrection continues to resonate powerfully within the hearts of millions, fostering a faith that is resilient, steadfast, and immoveable, and a hope that is unshakeable, inspiring tranquility in seemingly chaotic times and radiating spiritual strength in every situation.

Journal Exercise:

1. Revisit the narrative of the Crucifixion and Resurrection. In a couple of sentences, describe what these two events symbolize for your own faith journey.
2. Imagine yourself as one of the bystanders during the Crucifixion. What emotions and thoughts might you experience? How does this perspective deepen your understanding of the sacrifice made on the cross?
3. Reflect on the Resurrection as a demonstration of God's resilience and promise of eternal life. What does this mean for you in your personal life, your struggles, and your hopes?
4. Identify a moment in your life when you have experienced a form of 'resurrection', a moment of hope and renewal following hardship. How can this personal experience help you relate more deeply to the message of the resurrection story?

5. The Crucifixion and Resurrection bring attention to the power of faith and hope in dealing with life's trials. Write a brief prayer, expressing your gratitude for these gifts and seeking greater resilience in faith as you face your personal trials.

8
Letters of the New Testament

8.1 Pauline Letters: Theological Foundations

The epistles of Paul hold an eminent position in the New Testament, not only for their theological richness but also for their historical context that offers profound insights into the early Christian communities. To appreciate these letters fully, one must try to understand the socio-cultural and religious background during the first century AD, the time when Paul wrote them. During the first century AD, the Roman Empire flourished and dominated much of the Mediterranean world, including the regions where early Christian communities were emerging. The Greco-Roman culture influenced many facets of life, including language, education, politics, and religion. In most cities, Greek was the lingua franca and people worshipped a plethora of Greek and Roman gods. Against this backdrop, a small but growing group of believers, known as 'The Way' or later as Christians, dared to profess their faith in a single God and follow the teachings of a Jewish man named Jesus whom they proclaimed as their Messiah. These communities lived in a world where they were viewed with suspicion or hostility, sometimes facing persecutions. Their religious and moral principles deviated significantly from the societal norms of the Greco-Roman culture.

Paul, once a persecutor of Christians, became one of the most passionate proponents of Christianity after a profound conversion experience. By the time he started writing his letters, he had already undertaken several missionary journeys throughout Asia Minor and Europe, establishing Christian communities. These letters, addressed to specific communities or individuals, tackled theological issues, resolved disputes, provided moral guidelines, and encouraged believers in their faith journey. Paul's letters are valuable windows into the context of the early church, its struggles, and its resilient faith. Despite the volatile political and religious environment, these communities held a revolutionary belief, grounded in love, mercy, and the promise of the risen Christ. In their midst, we see the echoes of hope reverberating and faith demonstrating its resilience. In the broad narrative of Paul's letters, the historical and societal context is inseparable from the theological content. Knowing the context brings a richer understanding to the timeless spiritual truth Paul communicates - a truth that continues to resonate with us today. Drawing from Paul's letters to the early Christians, we dive deep into the exploration of ecclesiology and eschatology. Both these themes are monumental in understanding Christian faith and the hope that guides its practitioners.

If we examine Paul's epistles, the ecclesiology, or the study of the church, becomes evident as a significant theme. Paul's letters to the Corinthians and Ephesians, for example, provide distinct concepts of the church as the body of Christ. He imparts the image of believers as parts of a greater whole, each serving a unique purpose to contribute to the overall welfare and functioning of the church. Through this analogy, Paul emphasizes that diversity within unity is not just tolerable but necessary for the flourishing of the church. Simultaneously, he asks the members of this spiritual body to act out of love, selflessness, and dedication. Not against each other but towards the shared objective of glorifying God and His love for mankind. For instance, in his letter to the Ephesians (Eph 4:16), Paul says, "From whom the whole body, joined and held together by every joint with which it is equipped, when each part is working properly, makes the body grow so that it builds itself up in love." The importance of mutual care, respect, and affection within the church community is thus highlighted.

In parallel, Paul's writings also offer rich insight into eschatology - the doctrine of 'last things', or the ultimate destiny of humanity according to Christian belief. Throughout all his letters, both to individuals and communities, Paul continually reiterates the hope of an assured future in God's eternal kingdom. In 1 Thessalonians 4:13-18, Paul remarks on the Resurrection, a cornerstone of eschatology, comforting and encouraging the Thessalonians regarding those who have died in Christ. He reassures them that the deceased will rise again and meet the Lord in the air alongside those still living at Christ's return. It is a potent reminder that the end times should not incite fear but hope and joy because of God's promise of eternal life.

Paul's teachings on eschatology and ecclesiology intersect powerfully, utilizing the hope of a glorious future to encourage believers in their present. The Church, through its single yet diverse members working unison, is to take up the call to be Christ's representatives on earth. It should share the message of hope in the promise of God's eternal kingdom. This is the church's mission until Christ's eventual return. Here, ecclesiology and eschatology are not isolated doctrines but intertwined themes that paint a coherent narrative of profound hope, resilience, and the depiction of the church's journey. It's a journey fueled by the surety of a glorious future with God, cultivated through a community of believers committed to reflecting Christ's love. This is the resonance reflected throughout the Pauline epistles. An echo of hope that empowers us to live worthy lives while awaiting the promise of eternal bliss in God's kingdom. Writing in troubled times, Paul offers nourishment for every season. His letters create a comprehensive framework, encompassing the affirmation of current realities (the Church), the hopeful expectation of the future (eschatology), and the mutual interdependence between these two axes. The implications for believers like you and me is the urge to participate responsibly in the body of Christ for the glory of God and in anticipation of His return.

Letter	Date Written	Audience
Romans	57 AD	Church in Rome
1 Corinthians	53-54 AD	Church in Corinth
2 Corinthians	55-56 AD	Church in Corinth
Galatians	49-50 AD	Church in Galatia
Ephesians	60-61 AD	Church in Ephesus
Philippians	61-62 AD	Church in Philippi

Paul's letters, filled with unwavering faith and a resilient spirit, illustrate the transformative power of belief, providing valuable lessons for our fast-paced, complex modern lives. The fabric of Paul's teachings is woven of threads bearing the Siamese twins – resilience and hope, two qualities of faith that are essential for spiritual growth and sustenance. Let us traverse through the intricacies of this Pauline theology and uncover its unparalleled insights.

Firstly, we must acknowledge the relentless resolve that Paul embodied. Often seen as the apostle of adversity, he endured scourging, imprisonment, and incessant threats to his life. Yet, he embraced these tribulations as part of his transformational journey. Contrary to our instinctive reactions to problems – evasion or lament – Paul's stance teaches us to face adversity with grace and strength, recognizing and utilizing it as a vehicle to spiritual growth. In essence, each struggle we encounter is an opportunity to fortify our faith.

Secondly, the letters of Paul underline the seminal role of hope in maintaining our spiritual health. His unwavering hope in God's promises in the face of despair meant he continued to preach the Good News even when met with animosity and physical persecution. His hope came from a deeply rooted belief in the resurrection and the glorious future awaiting all believers. This profound, unwavering hope is a testament to Paul's faith and a beacon for us today, especially in times fraught with uncertainty.

Translating Paul's theology into our lives, resilience becomes our spiritual muscle, strengthened by exercise and tested in the face of trials. A resilient faith does not signify a problem-free existence; it instead equips us to take on struggles head-on, using them as catalysts to deepen our faith and grow more profound in our spiritual walk. Hope, according to Pauline theology, is an enriching virtue that lights up the path of faith. In our contemporary context, this hope infuses our lives with purpose, optimism, and peace, amid everyday churnings. Holding onto hope in God's promises ignites a positive outlook towards life, empowering us with the strength to surmount challenges, while instilling a serene sureness of God's providence.

In conclusion, Paul's life and writings invite us today to cultivate a resilient faith sufficient to buffer life's squalls, interweaved with an enduring hope that lights our path through darkness. This fusion of resilience and hope is the bedrock of Pauline theology, an essential supplement for our modern faith journey providing spiritual strength and tranquility. This indeed, is the echo of hope reverberating through Paul's teachings – an echo that, when heard and understood, has the power to transform our lives.

Journal Exercise:

1. Re-visit Paul's letters that we studied in this chapter. Which topics or themes spoke most profoundly to you today? Write it down and explain why.
2. Imagine having a conversation with Paul. What questions would you ask him based on your understanding and feelings towards his theological foundations? Record these questions.

3. Now, attempt to answer these questions yourself based on what you've learnt and comprehended from this chapter.
4. Drawing from the wisdom of Paul's theological foundations, how can these principles apply to a personal situation or challenge that you are facing or have faced recently?
5. Write a letter to your future self, summarizing what you learned from Pauline Theology today and how you intend to implement those principles in your daily life.

With each entry, remember to date your responses for future reflection.

8.2 James: Faith and Works

Indeed, the Book of James offers a spectacular delineation of the relationship between faith and works. James, the brother of Jesus, is the writer of this book who deftly discusses the synergy of faith and works that should characterize the life of a Christian believer. Faith and works are two sides of the same coin in the Christian life, each feeding into and strengthening the other. One cannot exist without the other, and both are essential to living a life honoring God. With the apostle James as our guide, we see evidence of this relationship through various examples in his book:

Firstly, in James 2:14-26, he vividly explored the necessity of faith being accompanied by actions. He stated, "What does it profit, my brethren, if someone says he has faith but does not have works? Can faith save him?" (James 2:14). He further argued that faith without works is dead, using the actions of Abraham and Rahab as illustrations. Abraham's belief in God was marked by his willingness to offer his son Isaac on the altar. Rahab's faith in God led her to protect the Israelite spies.

Secondly, James emphasized that true faith produces good works. In James 1:22, he advised against being mere listeners of the word and instead encouraged to be doers of the word. James insisted on the obedient action, which bridges the gap between listening to God's word and doing what it says.

Lastly, James went on to illustrate that works also enrich our faith. In James 1:25, he compared a person who takes heed to the word and does what it says to a man who looks into a mirror, continues in it, and is blessed. Here, he used the metaphor of a mirror to describe God's word. As one delves deeper into his Word, it reflects their true spiritual state, instigating transformation and consequently the production of good works.

We see in the book of James that faith and works are not mutually exclusive but rather two interconnected facets of Christian life. The faith that saves is the faith that works. And these works, produced by faith, serve to fortify faith. It's a beautiful tandem which carries a profound truth: Our faith in God should produce good works, and these good works should reflect back on and strengthen our faith. Understanding this concept of the interplay between faith and works in the Book of James aids us in navigating the complexities of our Christian journey in a modern world fraught with challenges. This helps establish a resilient faith, one equipped to handle both personal and collective trials.

James, the brother of Jesus, offers remarkable insights into the resilience of faith that still resonate today. His teachings, captured in the New Testament, provide valuable perspectives on faith, perseverance, and spirituality. Indeed, James's first premise that calls for special attention is pertaining to how the adversities of life serve to strengthen faith. In James 1:2-4, "Consider it pure joy, my brothers and sisters, whenever you face trials of many kinds, because you know that the testing of your faith produces perseverance..." This notion positions the testing of faith not as a destructive force, but rather as a transformative one that fosters tenacity, thus implying a resilient nature of faith.

From a modern perspective, this may mean that life's troubles–be they financial, relational, emotional, or even spiritual struggles–are not obstacles, but opportunities to bolster one's faith. In such a context, resilience becomes the key to unlocking the transformative power of faith. Recognizing that challenge breeds growth can then lead to a spiritual awakening and renewed hope. Furthermore, James exhorts us towards action in conjunction to faith. In James 2:17, he declares, "In the same way, faith by itself, if it is not accompanied by action, is dead." This highlights that faith is not passive; it is an active engagement with God's word and requires action to manifest its impact. This interplay between faith and action reinforces the resilience of faith through active engagement with hardships that it serves to conquer. In a modern light, this might translate into a call to action in times of difficulties. Rather than relinquishing our agency under the crushing weight of troubles, it could mean picking up our proverbial staff and venturing forth on the uncertain path with resolute faith and determined action.

Lastly, James professes an intriguing link between wisdom and unwavering faith in James 1:5-8. He advises that anyone lacking wisdom should ask God, "who gives generously to all without finding fault, and it will be given to them". However, the request must be made in faith, with no doubt, for the one who doubts is like a wave of the sea, blown and tossed by the wind. This suggests that seeking wisdom from God is essential to strengthen faith and its resilience. It also warns against doubting, which may cloud faith's clarity and stir confusion, impairing one's steadfastness. The unwavering faith earnestly seeking God's wisdom resonates as resilient faith in the face of trials.

In the tapestry of modern living, this could possibly be a reminder to seek God's wisdom when we face dilemmas or crossroads, and to do so with a trust that doesn't waiver. Our faith's resilience grows as we meet our personal wisdom with divine insight, allowing us to navigate life's tumultuous seas with a steadfastness that propels us forward rather than letting us drift along the waves. James's teachings hence offer avenues for deeper understanding of the resilient nature of faith. They motivate a shift in perception towards trials, encourage active involvement of faith, and promote the seeking of wisdom from God to nurture and hone the resilience of faith. Through his lens, we can then comprehend how faith becomes a beacon of hope, shining light onto the dark corners of our greatest challenges, and empowering us to emerge stronger.

In James' teachings, there is a profound message regarding faith and works. Building on this understanding, we can start applying these insights into promoting spiritual strength and modern serenity in our everyday lives. Firstly, the notion of works is not confined to the physical labor we carry out daily. It also includes acts of kindness, compassion, love, and other virtues that exemplify a Christ-like character. These are soul-soothing activities that bring tranquility and peace into our live, even for a moment in this chaotic modern world.

- Expressing love and forgiveness: In James 2:8, it reads about the Royal law found in Scripture, "Love your neighbor as yourself." Love is not just a feeling but an active expression. In a modern context, this can be as simple as offering help to those who need it, lending an empathetic ear to those who are burdened, or forgiving others and ourselves for our shortcomings.
- Nurturing Inner Strength: James 1:3 reveals the truth about trials and tribulations - "You know that the testing of your faith produces

perseverance." This speaks well to resilience, an essential quality for coping with the ups and downs of the modern world. It suggests that every adversity can be an opportunity to develop inner strength, if viewed from the perspective of faith.

- Peacemaking: In James 3:18, peacemakers "who sow in peace reap a harvest of righteousness." This shows how important it is to promote peace in our interactions and decisions. Creating a peaceful environment at work, at home, or within our social circle, fosters serenity and spiritual well-being.
- Prioritizing the Word: One of the most beneficial activities we can do to find inner tranquility and cultivate spiritual strength is by making it a point to study the word of God. James 1:22 urges us, "Do not merely listen to the word, and so deceive yourselves. Do what it says." This doesn't just refer to Bible studies but includes integrating God's teachings into our daily life - in our choices, interactions, and mindsets.
- Practicing humility: James suggests that humility is an essential aspect of our spiritual journey. James 4:10 reads, "Humble yourselves before the Lord, and he will lift you up." In a world often fueled by ego and competition, practicing humility provides a sense of tranquility and peace.

At the end of the day, faith and works should not be viewed as separate aspects of our spiritual lives. Rather, they should intertwine, much like the roots of a tree. As seen in James 2:26, "As the body without the spirit is dead, so faith without deeds is dead." By integrating faith into our actions - our 'works' - we breathe life into our beliefs, nurturing our spiritual strength and developing a peaceful and serene heart.

8.3 Peter: Lessons in Spiritual Resilience

Immersing ourselves into the world of the New Testament, we stumble upon the charismatic character of Peter. A prominent figure, he gestates as a raw, open book of emotions, faith, and frailty, developing into a tower of strength that instigates the establishment of the Church. His life echoes the resilience of faith that can serve as a beacon for us to find modern serenity and spiritual strength. Born as Simon (Matthew 4:18), Peter was a Galilean fisherman, outlined by the roughness of his vocation. His life underwent a profound change when he accepted Jesus' simple invitation, "Follow me. I will make you fishers of men" (Matthew 4:19). From that moment, the journey of Peter mirrors a quest of self-transformation and growing faith. Peter had many encounters with Jesus that shaped his faith and impressionable character. Certain events stood out like the miracle on Lake Genessart (Luke 5:1-11), where Jesus filled his nets with an overwhelming catch. It was upon seeing this miracle that Peter confessed his unworthiness in the face of the divine and was reassured by Jesus of his new path.

We witness Peter's faith evolve in leaps and bounds at the extraordinary confession at Caesarea Philippi (Matthew 16:13-20). Here, Peter becomes the first to recognize Jesus as the Christ, the Son of the Living God. It is then that Jesus rechristens Simon as Peter, the rock on which His Church would be built. The strength of Peter's faith leads him to make such a profound acknowledgment before the other disciples, underscoring his spiritual growth. However, Peter was also a man of frailties; he falters in his faith. Amid the tempest on the sea (Matthew 14:22-32), as he attempts to walk on the water toward Jesus, he doubts, resulting in his near-drowning. Yet, Jesus does not chastise Peter; instead, he extends his hand to save him, illustrating how faith, even when it wavers, is met with divine mercy.

Witnessing Jesus' Transfiguration, Peter exhibits his characteristic impetuosity by suggesting the erection of three tabernacles (Matthew 17:1-9). He fails to comprehend that he was to witness Moses and Elijah passing on the baton of their prophetic mission to Jesus, not to equate all three. Yet, this incident gives us an insight into Peter's eagerness and his willingness to act on his convictions, making us relate to him even more keenly. The last supper offers a glimpse into Peter's loyalty towards Jesus when he vehemently professes his readiness to die with him (Matthew 26:35). However, within hours, he succumbs to his fear and denies knowing Jesus, a painful prediction prophetically made by Jesus himself (Matthew 26:75). But his subsequent sorrow manifested his great love that refused to dwell in the abyss of denial, prompting a resurrection of his faith. Post-resurrection, Peter reaffirms his love for Jesus three times (John 21:15-17), symbolizing a divine redemption of his three-fold denial. As Jesus entrusts him with the shepherd's task, we see Peter transfiguring into a leader, poised to guide the early church with his faith. Despite his shortcomings and errors, Peter emerges as a rock-solid pillar of faith. In his growth from a humble fisherman to a backbone of the early Church, we find echoes of hope and inspiration. Peter's life serves as a rich reservoir of lessons on faith's resilience, capable of fostering spiritual strength in our modern lives. Understanding his context and character indeed provides a deep comprehension of faith in unfailing divine mercy and love.

Peter, one of the chosen apostles and a cornerstone of the early Church, faced various trials throughout his life, which inextricably shaped his faith journey. Particularly, the key events in Peter's life provide a mirror on experiencing trials, their impact, and the eventual triumph and resilience of faith. In Matthew 14:22-33, the narrative shows Peter attempting to walk on water. He called out to Jesus, initially displaying confidence and walking upon the waters. However, as fear gripped him, he began to sink but was saved by Jesus, who reached out and pulled him to safety. This event depicts fear as a common human frailty that can make faith waver. Yet, the redeeming power of God's grace, represented by Jesus' hand pulling Peter out of the water, demonstrates that even when faith weakens, His love is still readily available to rescue and restore us. Then, we see Peter during the Transfiguration of Jesus in Matthew 17:1-9. Here, the apostle witnesses the divine glory of Jesus and offers to build shelters for Jesus, Moses, and Elijah, clearly in awe of such a spectacle. Peter's reaction illustrates our natural desire to capture and hold onto awe-inspiring moments, which are often signs of God's presence and grace. This teaches us that faith isn't only about holding on during difficulties, but also recognizing grace in divine moments of revelation and using these moments to strengthen and build resilience.

Another fundamental event in Peter's faith journey is his denial of Jesus during His trial (Luke 22:54-62). As prophesied by Jesus, Peter denied Him three times before the rooster crowed. Overwhelmed by guilt, Peter wept bitterly. The apostle's denials were likely precipitated by fear and confusion, but they also depicted a low point in his faith journey, where he temporarily loses sight of truth and loyalty. Nevertheless, despite his failings, Peter's story didn't end in this regrettable denial. He was ultimately restored and strengthened by Jesus after His resurrection, proving that trials and failures can collectively contribute to the resilience and maturation of faith. Lastly, in John 21:15-19, post-resurrection, Jesus forgives Peter and reaffirms his role to "feed His sheep". Here Jesus, instead of condemning Peter's failures, reinstates him in his role and, even more, entrusts him with the responsibility of shepherding His people. This restoration was significant as it not only portrayed God's ability to forgive and renew but also detailed how past failings need not mar our future service and commitment. In conclusion, Peter's trials and triumphs exemplify the different stages of a faith journey that we too may walk through. Fear, awe of God's power, the pain of disloyalty, and the joy of forgiveness are all part of this journey. Peter's life story is a powerful testament to the inextricable link between trials and spiritual resilience. His character transformation from a fear-stricken denier to influential Church leader serves as a beacon of hope, reminding us that, amidst trials, we should not lose heart. We are constantly being shaped, forgivable, and able to build resilience held together by the inexhaustible grace of God.

Peter's life, as chronicled in the Bible, offers an abundance of lessons that readers can leverage to cultivate serenity and spiritual strength. His story demonstrates that faith is not static; it grows and evolves with time, containing highs and lows that are inherent to the human experience. His journey and transformation into a pillar of the early church provide us with insights that are particularly relevant in the modern world.

Firstly, faith, like Peter's, involves progressively deepening trust. Peter was introduced as a simple fisherman. He was not a warrior nor was he a scholar. Yet, he was willing to leave his life behind to follow Jesus, confident that something valuable awaited him. This marks the beginning of his journey of faith. His departure from the familiar challenges us to loosen our grip on physical, material pursuits and reorient our focus on cultivating spiritual depth. On our own journeys, we might face situations where our faith is called to the forefront, situations that seem impractical or illogical in the natural order of things. Like Peter in the stormy seas, we have the choice to step out despite our fears. By doing so, we channel our faith from the intellectual realms into our actions. Even when we falter, as Peter did, we are reminded that faith is not triumphing over waves every time, but trusting the hand that reaches out to us when we sink.

Secondly, Peter's faith was marked by his willingness to confess his love and acceptance of the gospel, in spite of the potential risks associated with the declaration. This dedication to truth and his oneness with spirit, even when it seemed inconvenient, is a fundamental lesson. Fears and societal pressures may push us into closets of conformity. But stepping out, speaking up for our beliefs, and staying true to our faith, can build spiritual resilience. Our heart-felt confessions, even when manifested in whispers, can generate ripples of change.

Lastly, one of the most poignant examples of spiritual strength was demonstrated in Peter's encounter with failure. Upon denying Jesus three times, one might think of this as the end of his spiritual journey. Yet, he wept, he repented, and he was restored. This showcases an overlooked aspect of faith – an ability to embrace failure, process guilt, and bounce back. Seeing failure as a spiritual checkpoint and not as a dead-end can diffuse the negative emotions, helping us reclaim our serenity. Peter's life is evocative of a faith that accepted its imperfections. His spiritual robustness was not built in a day but was a testament to his continual strive towards spiritual growth. Examining his life, the echo of hope becomes clear – faith can be resilient, even in the face of adversity. It is this kind of faith, embodied by Peter, that we are encouraged to emulate to cultivate modern serenity and spiritual strength.

Lesson Number	Key Point	Reflection
1	Acceptance in turmoil	Growth through struggle
2	Humility in power	Understanding the purpose of strength
3	Surrender in resistance	Finding peace in acceptance
4	Faith amidst doubt	Believing in unseen
5	Love in hatred	Overcoming adversity with kindness
6	Prayer in solitude	Connection with divine in isolation

Journal Exercise:

Begin by listing three challenges you believe that Peter faced in his journey. Beside each one, outline how his faith may have played a role in overcoming them. From your analysis of Peter's experiences, list two to three ways you believe you can emulate his spiritual resilience in your own life's challenges. Reflect on a recent challenge you faced. How could Peter's faith-inspired responses be applied to your situation? Record any insights or realizations you gain from this reflection. Take a moment to write a short prayer or affirmation inspired by Peter's resilience to support your own spiritual strength.

9
Conclusion

9.1 Synthesizing the Lessons: The Journey Thus Far

As we open the sacred pages of the Bible, we encounter stories brimming with the resilience of faith, testament to the strength and power of believing, even and especially, in the midst of struggle and strife. Let me take you back on a journey through some of these remarkable narratives.

Firstly, journeying through the book of Genesis, we come across the compelling story of Noah. A man described as a faultless person in his generation, Noah found favor in the eyes of the Lord. Living in a world filled with wickedness, he held firm to his faith, obeying God's command to build an ark for the saving of his household. The feat of this construction, the ridicule he must have received, the loneliness of standing against the tide – these are frustrations we can only start to fathom. But through it all, Noah exhibited faith resilient enough to withstand the test of the times.

Secondly, we retrieve the account of Abraham, famously called the Father of Faith. Abraham is remembered for his unwavering confidence in God's promises, despite their seeming improbability. In the face of barrenness, age, and an uncertain journey, Abraham's faith did not waver. He did not waver through unbelief regarding the promise of God but was strengthened in his faith and gave glory to God, being fully convinced that God was able to do what he had promised. This deep trust anchored Abraham, forming the bedrock of the resilience we wish to capture.

Thirdly, the story of Job is one that starkly stands out in this collection. A prosperous man struck with enduring calamities, Job's faith was put through the ultimate test. His friends and wife incited him to curse God and die. However, even amidst his anguish and confusion, Job resolved, "Though he slay me, yet will I trust in Him." This profound declaration is the quintessence of resilient faith.

Lastly, but certainly not least, we consider the struggles and resilience of the Apostle Paul. Persecuted, beaten, imprisoned, yet relentlessly pressing on, Paul's journey is a testament to the resilience of faith. He reminds us to rejoice in our sufferings, knowing that suffering produces endurance, endurance produces character, and character produces hope. An echo resounding through the ages, imploring us to never surrender our faith, no matter how dire the circumstances.

By revisiting these pieces of the grand biblical tapestry, we glean renewed insights into faith's resilience and the ways we might cultivate it for our modern lives.

Key Insight	Learning	Future Scope
Engaging narrative	Simplified complex concepts	Engage with more complexity
Diverse perspectives	Enhanced critical thinking	Include more perspectives
Conceptual depth	Deepened understanding	Study further nuances
Interactive content	Increased engagement	Build more interactive elements
Structured learning	Improved comprehension	Streamline learning journey
Personal growth	Appreciated value of learning	Continue personal development

In today's fast-paced world, the pursuit of modern serenity often seems like an elusive dream rather than an attainable reality. Society burdens us with expectations and obligations which leave us in the constant chase of unending goals. Yet, when we turn to the pages of ancient scriptures, we are able to unearth timeless principles that foster a sense of serenity in this chaotic modern era.

Let's delve into some core teachings of the scriptures which guide us toward embracing contemporary calm. Firstly, the concept of acceptance plays a pivotal role. Many scriptural accounts illustrate how various figures accepted their circumstances, even those that were unfavorable, with grace and courage. A key to achieving tranquility lies not in avoiding life's storms but in learning to dance in the rain.

Secondly, scriptures underscore the importance of faith in shaping our outlook toward life. Faith encourages us to trust in divine guidance, thus reducing anxiety built from uncertainty. Noah's ark, for instance, was built not on scientific foresight, but on unyielding faith. This shows that often serenity comes from trusting the journey, even when we cannot see the destination.

Thirdly, forgiveness, a principle repeated numerous times throughout the scriptures, acts as a cleanse for the soul. It does not alter the past, but it does open up a future. From the story of the Prodigal son to Jesus on the cross, forgiveness continues to be advocated as a path to peace.

Moreover, the scriptures teach us the intrinsic value of gratitude. Whether it was Jesus thanking the Father for loaves and fishes before feeding thousands, or Paul speaking of contentment in every situation, the recognition of blessings, even in meager amounts, echoes loudly throughout the holy text. In our modern day, psychologists confirm that a daily practice of gratitude enhances emotional well-being, bringing us closer to a state of serenity.

Lastly, the practice of unconditional love, demonstrated by Christ willingly laying down his life, serves as an lodestar for achieving modern serenity. Empathy and love towards others reduce conflict and foster a sense of interconnectedness, vital for psychological tranquility.

We are given explicit instructions, principles, teachings, and guidance through the divine narrations, but it is upon us to decipher, interpret, and mold them into our contemporary framework. Spiritual resilience, thus, is not merely about overcoming adversity but learning and growing from the experience, as these narratives vividly depict. In understanding these themes, we gradually shift our perspective from a stressful and troubled mentality to one filled with hope, serenity, and peace—a peaceful echo resonating back through timeless scriptures, providing a fundamental framework for living a tranquil life in our modern era. It is incumbent upon us to seek out such echoes of hope in the scripture's ancient narratives, carrying their wisdom into our own journeys and daily lives.

Rooted from our shared exploration in the earlier sections, one of the key resources that hold the potential to strengthen our faith and help us navigate through adversities is the fusion of biblical wisdom and confronting modern challenges. Here's a closer look at how we, in today's world, can unearth spiritual tenacity by surveying these narratives:

Diving into the narrative of Job, his unwavering faith despite extensive suffering is one area we can draw inspiration from. When facing trials and tribulations, we often question God's intentions or doubt His existence, but in Job's story, we see persistence. He never denounced God, and this steadfast faith eventually brought about blessings and restoration - a pointer to the brand of resilience we ought to have.

Consider also the story of Joseph – wronged by his brothers, sold into slavery, wrongly accused and imprisoned. Yet, he held firm to his faith, a spiritual strength ebbed from it. When opportunities arose, Joseph was highly positioned in Egypt, essentially saving his family in the course of a severe famine. The trials served as stepping stones closer to his purpose. They prepared him for a higher assignment. Analogous to Joseph's struggles, challenges in the contemporary world don't necessarily have to trigger doubt or loss of faith; rather, they should challenge us to recognize God's purpose and stand firm in our conviction.

Notice furthermore how Moses responded to his mission to deliver the Israelites from slavery in Egypt. Initial doubt and fear held him captive, but when he chose faith over fear, God empowered him to perform great miracles. The magnitude of our modern dilemmas can indeed be daunting. The bills piling up, relationships dwindling, joblessness hitting hard– they may seem insurmountable. But, with an unwearied spirit rooted deeply in faith, it's remarkable what can be accomplished.

Whilst these narratives engulf varying degrees and types of challenges, their unity lies in one single facet–faith's resilience. The narratives stimulate mindfulness about what faith looked like in the biblical era, while embracing and confronting modern-day challenges can infectiously impact our spiritual strength.

Here are key lessons we can derive:

- Faith's resilience isn't developed in the absence of adversity but within it: Like Job, Joseph, and Moses, our faith is refined through our struggles. The heartache, disappointments, and adversities aren't intended to cripple us; instead, they strengthen our faith – making us more resilient.

- Stay Rooted in God, even when faced with the unthinkable: Your trials might shake you, but don't let them uproot you from your faith. Be like Job, who, even when he lost everything, never lost his faith in God.
- Your trials might just be a stepping stone to your destiny: Joseph ascended to a higher purpose through his trials. Your trials, however heartbreaking they may be, could be leading you to a greater path that God has designed specifically for you.

As you pause to reflect on faith's resilience and commit to maintaining a strong spirit amidst life's turbulence, you would ideally glean embraced tranquility in engaging with adversities and derive strength for the journey. What we see as a mountain may just be a stepping stone.

Journal Exercise:

1. Write down the three most impactful lessons you've extrapolated through this journey of faith resilience study. Why did these lessons resonate with you the most?
2. Select a Bible story that peeks your interests. Reflect and identify how the protagonist in the story demonstrates faith resilience.
3. How has your understanding and perspective on faith resilience evolved after completing this study? Share some personal changes you've noticed - it can be a change in mindset, behavior, or attitude.
4. Envision a future challenge you might face in your life. Drawing upon the lessons learned, write a blueprint on how you'll use your spiritual strength to navigate through it.
5. Lastly, express your gratitude and write a thanksgiving prayer. This prayer should shed light upon what you're grateful for, the wisdom you've gained, and the growth you've experienced through this study. Remember, gratitude multiplies the good in life and also fortifies our faith resilience.

Remember to spend a quiet moment of reflection after writing to let these insights sink in. You are encouraged to return to your entries in the future to see your spiritual growth.

9.2 Spiritual Practices for Resilient Faith

A resilient faith quite often swings on the hinges of habitual spiritual disciplines. These intentional actions, when consistently practiced, form the bedrock of spiritual resilience in an ever-changing environment, ensuring you are grounded, steadfast, and ever growing in faith. Let us prove to ourselves how these rituals are found in the Bible and then provide a guide on how incorporating them in our daily lives can significantly transform and strengthen our faith.

Moses, an exceptional figure in Biblical history, was a disciplined man. He maintained his intimate relationship with God by persistently meeting with Him on a mountain – a practice that ultimately led to the deliverance of the Israelites from slavery. We learn from Exodus 34:4-5 that Moses, in his resilience, broke the walls of the possible with his continuous dedication to prayer. It was during these solitary periods of connection that God gave Moses instructions, proving that scheduled spiritual rituals like prayer can be conduits for receiving direction and spiritual growth.

There's also Daniel, a captive in Babylon, whose unwavering faith in God arose from his unfailing spiritual rituals. Directed by his resolve and uncompromising personal disciplines, he prayed three times a day, despite the decree against any form of worship, risking the lion's den matters tended to end in his favor and he remained steadfast (Daniel 6:10-28). His spiritual resilience was anchored in the power of habit. Daniel's story is a clear indication that consistent spiritual rituals can form a fortress around our faith, we become resilient even when adversity strikes.

Yet, sometimes, these spiritual practices may not come naturally to us. That's okay. It is a process, an exercise, much like physical training, that requires commitment, time, and dedication. Here are some recommended daily habits to cultivate for fortitude in faith:

1. Prayer and Meditation: This discipline is a channel of communication with God, urging us onward in faith, requiring our quietness before Him to hear his guidance.
2. Reading and Reflecting on Scriptures: This is food for the soul. Make it a habit to meditate on what you have read and ask God for understanding.
3. Journaling: This allows you to pen down your thoughts, your prayers, God's promptings, and answers. It also helps you keep

track of your spiritual growth and understand the patterns of God's work in your life.

4. Worship: A great way to begin and end your day. Praises lift your spirit and create an atmosphere conducive to God's presence.
5. Silent Moments: These are unique periods of quietness where you can listen, decipher and understand what God is communicating.
6. Service to Others: Actively serving and loving others can be a beneficial spiritual discipline. It reminds us of Christ's deed and helps us emulate His love for humanity.

Incorporating these habits into your daily life will not happen overnight. Allow yourself the grace to gradually expand them into your routine, recognizing that even minor changes can contribute to major spiritual growth. Keep in mind; spiritual resilience does not equate to perfection. It's about progress and striving to build a deeper relationship with God each day.

It was within the solitude and silence of the Garden of Gethsemane, under the eerie glow of a dim moon, that Jesus demonstrated the depth of his profound connection with the Father. Alone and in prayer, he found the strength to bear the weight of the impending cross. His solemn plea projected a model of resilience found only in Sacred Conversations. Just as Jesus found comfort and strength in prayer, we must also seek solace and fortify our faith within our intimate dialogues with God. In this sacred space, the whispers of our heart meet divinity, our fears transform into fortitudes, and we find our resilience being built brick by emotional brick.

- Praying is being vulnerable before God. In solitude, we lay bare our hearts, and in the unwavering purity of our raw emotions, there is an uncanny strength. In crying out, as David did in Psalms or Hannah in her plea for a son in 1 Samuel1:10, faith is tested and solidified.
- Praying is seeking divine guidance. Just as the Wise Men sought directions to Bethlehem via divine connections, prayer provides a spiritual compass that aligns our steps in accordance to God's plan. When we surrender our understanding and self-will, we gain spiritual strength, allowing the resonance of divine wisdom to guide us.
- Praying is complete reliance on God's provision. Supplying thousands with only five loaves and two fishes as shown in the story of the multiplication is a stark reminder of God's boundless provision. Our

prayers of supplication echo into the halls of heaven, reshaping our perception of our limitations and building resilience.

- Praying is intercession. Abraham's plea for Sodom in Genesis 18 is a vigorous demonstration of advocacy that interchanges between standing in the gap for others and reaping spiritual strength. When we pray for others, the selfless act of intercession reinforces our resilience.
- Praying is an act of worship. From Moses' songs of praise at the shores of the Red Sea to Jesus' words of surrender in Gethsemane, prayer transcends our individual needs and bears testament to our awe, reverence, and submission to God's sovereignty. As we continuously commune with God, wrapped in the invisible spiritual tapestry that binds our hearts with the divine, we rumble with life's challenges, we strengthen our faith muscles, and we build resilience. Resilience, after all, is not just our ability to weather life's adversities but also, it is in our capacity to grow in spite of them. It's not about bouncing back, but rather bouncing forward.

Just like the Biblical figures before us — Job who never lost his faith despite his immeasurable suffering, Joseph who stood steadfast despite his tribulations, and even Jesus, who despite his humanity, held onto his divine purpose up to his last breath — they all harnessed the power of prayer, turning their sacred conversations into a sanctuary of spiritual strength. Faith's resilience, therefore, is nourished within these sacred conversations. It grows in the fertile ground of genuine connection, of surrender, of trust. In prayer, we find not only a way to cope but rather a wellspring of strength, a home of peace, and a haven of hope, echoing through the seemingly endless chaotic chambers of life.

Practice Type	Duration	Benefits
Meditation	30 minutes daily	Boosts mindfulness
Prayer	Varies	Enhances spiritual connection
Fasting	Bi-weekly	Promotes discipline
Scripture Reading	20 minutes daily	Enhances knowledge
Nature Walks	Weekly	Promotes physical health

Practice Type	Duration	Benefits
Service to Others	As opportunities arise	Builds empathy

In a world that is continually shifting and often full of uncertainty, the Word of God provides an unchanging foundation upon which we can build our lives. This divine Word is not only meant to be read or heard but to be actively studied and applied in our day-to-day lives. It's intended to be our guide, our go-to solution, our source of peace, wisdom, and spiritual strength. The Scriptures share wisdom and encouragement, irrespective of whom we are or the century we live within. The trials faced in the Bible hold lessons that are fundamentally relevant and applicable in the modern world — demonstrating God's unchanging love and faithfulness in adversity.

From the onset, our role involves maintaining an intentional attitude to Scripture. Here's how we can integrate God's Word into daily living for modern serenity:

- Meditate on the Word: Consider making biblical meditation a regular part of your spiritual regimen. This form of meditation involves pondering God's Word, reflecting on its relevance, and trying to gain deeper insights. This practice can entail memorizing verses, reciting them, and thinking deeply about their meaning. This form of meditation opens our minds and hearts to the Holy Spirit's guidance, allowing us to understand the scriptures profoundly.
- Apply the Scriptures: With an understanding of God's Word, we need to actively apply its teachings in our lives. Imagine each biblical teaching as a prism through which to view our actions, decisions, and attitudes. For instance, we can apply "Love your neighbor as yourself" by showing kindness to others, irrespective of their background. Applying these teachings fosters love, peace, unity, and patience, all essential for serenity in our modern world.
- Keep His Word close: Carry His contrasts or truths with you literally and figuratively. Write down your favorite comforting verses and keep them in places where you'll regularly see them, such as your workspace or on your fridge. Having God's Word ever-present acts as a reminder of His unfailing love and promise of peace.
- Use the Word as a tool for prayer: Using the scriptures as a template for prayer puts us in line with God's will and purpose. You can use the Psalms, the Lord's Prayer, or Paul's prayers in the Epistles to guide you.

When you align your prayers with the Word of God, it helps cultivate an environment where peace, joy, and hope can thrive.

- Encourage others with the Word: Sharing and discussing the scriptures with friends and family creates a nurturing, loving, and peaceful environment. It extends the impact of God's Word from your life to others, building a community of harmony and serenity.

Lastly, persistently applying God's Word promotes an active faith that doesn't easily waver in the face of life's uncertainties. Immersing in His Word allows our spirits to strengthen, causing us to rise above challenging circumstances and radiate faith, joy, and serenity. The Scriptures aren't only a record of God's word from centuries past. It's a treasure chest of guidance, consolation, correction, and inspiration for today and all tomorrows. For modern serenity and spiritual strength, open this chest and employ its riches in your life journey.

Journal Exercise:

Begin by listing down the spiritual practices discussed in this chapter that resonate with you most. Write about how you are currently incorporating these practices in your daily life or how you plan to do so in the future.

Reflect on a moment of hardship you encountered and describe how these spiritual practices could have helped or did help you build resilient faith during that time.

Next, consider how these practices can further strengthen your faith and provide serenity in the face of future challenges.

Also, jot down three Bible verses or stories from this or previous chapters that you can turn to as reminders of resilient faith when you encounter future trials.

Lastly, write a personal commitment based on your understanding and reflections, stating how you intend to grow and maintain your resilient faith by further adopting these spiritual practices.

9.3 Future Directions for Study

When we immerse ourselves in the profound depths of Biblical narratives, we often encounter situations, dilemmas, and moral quandaries that may feel far removed from our day-to-day experiences. Yet, just because the setting or cultural context is vastly different, it does not mean that the principles cannot be applied to address contemporary issues. The nexus of ancient wisdom and modern predicaments is where we find the true essence of Bible's teachings, a shimmering beacon of guidance enabling us to navigate the ever-evolving landscape of our lives. Take for instance the story of Joseph and his brothers in Egypt. An epitome of resilience, Joseph's life is a distinctive map that we can use to navigate our way through bouts of jealousy, betrayal, and redemption. His story, punctuated by pitfalls and victories, offers valuable insights into handling personal trauma and hardship, underlining the significance of forgiveness and perseverance.

Similarly, the classic narrative of David and Goliath encourages us to face our giants, both those visible and invisible. In our contemporary context, these might include issues such as mental health struggles, financial pressure, or societal injustice. Despite the magnitude of the challenge, we are reminded of the efficacy of faith, strategy, and courage to overcome seemingly insurmountable obstacles. Just as David, armed with a simple slingshot, was able to topple the giants, we too, carrying the symbolic weapons of prayer, faith, and action, can conquer our modern-day giants.

In our exploration of gender roles and equality, the Bible provides debatable but enlightening perspectives. We encounter women like Ruth, Deborah, and Esther, who exhibited remarkable leadership, courage, and dedication during their respective times. In Ruth, we see a symbol of steadfast loyalty; in Deborah, we find a model of wise leadership, and Esther stands as a resounding testament to courage and faith in the face of seemingly insurmountable societal challenges.

Lastly, we decipher the teachings of the Bible for offering guidance in today's digital age. The Ten Commandments may not explicitly discuss technology, but the ethical and moral principles it presents can be extrapolated to address issues such as online privacy, cyber bullying, and digital addiction. By leveraging the timeless wisdom embedded in these guidelines, we can navigate and interact with cyber technologies responsibly and graciously. In conclusion, by deeply mining the Bible for its universal truths, wisdom, and guiding principles, we can successfully tackle many pressing contemporary issues. The ancient narratives, although crafted in a different era, hold potent solutions for modern complications, making the Bible an indomitable fortress of guidance and hope.

Research Topic	Methods	Expected Outcomes
Genomic Sequencing	Next-Generation Sequencing	Novel Genetic Markers
Climate Change Modeling	Simulations	Future Climate Predictions
Artificial Intelligence	Machine Learning Algorithms	Advancements in AI
Renewable Energies	Experimentation	Enhanced Energy Sources
Nano Technology	Material Characterization	Improved Materials
Human Psychology	Neuroimaging	Brain Function Insights

Diving into the modern applications of traditional Christian values from Bible stories, we approach faithfulness as one of the stellar virtues relentlessly promoted in the scriptures. Rooted in trust and devotion, faithfulness has manifested in several forms in numerous Bible stories. The formidable resilience of those who promulgated steadfast dedication often leaves us in a sense of awe, guiding us to unearth our own tenacity in the face of adversity. Understanding the concept of faithfulness from the Bible, we draw parallels from its text to our modern world. Intricately woven into the fabric of our daily lives, these Biblical lessons resonate with our struggles, our triumphs, our decisions, and even our very own existential crises.

- The story of Noah and the ark is a testament to unyielding faithfulness amid ridicule and disbelief. Noah's belief in God's words and his resolute commitment to his task carved a path of survival and hope. Modern application of this Biblical truth encourages asserting our faith in the face of adversity, nurturing a solution-oriented mindset even when sailing alone amidst a world brimming with cynicism.
- Daniel in the lion's den is yet another portrayal of steadfast faith. His unflinching commitment towards his prayers, defying the King's law, only to be protected from the lions by his faith, challenges us to hold

onto our values, irrespective of the external pressure and prevailing societal norms.

- The story of Ruth and Naomi lays bare the power of loyalty as a form of resilience. Ruth's humane and devoted posture towards her desolate mother-in-law grounded in faith, rose above base survival instincts. Modern application translates to maintaining our relationships faithfully, especially during times of distress, moving beyond self-interest, to love unconditionally.

These timeless stories rediscovered in today's setting bridge a connection between then and now. They embolden us to choose faith over fear, resilience over retreat, in our pursuit of serenity and spiritual strength. Moreover, emulating the resilience of Biblical models requires recognizing the significance of faith as an enduring force. Embracing faithfulness is about making a conscious choice to draw strength from divine wisdom and love.

As we strive to walk on the path of faithfulness, it's important to remember that the advent of faithfulness is a continuous journey. It's not a static destination but an evolving process, engraved in ordinary decisions that showcase our commitment towards the divine, towards others, and towards our own inner being. Just as beauty uncovers in every echo of resilience, this journey sparks the advent of hope, broadening our horizon of faith. The Bible, with its impactful portrayals, empowers us to find our voice amidst the echoes of hope, shaping an avenue of resilience to live with compassion, integrity, and above all, unerring faithfulness. Ultimately, faithfulness is the silent prayer that keeps the resilient spirit alive - a powerful echo that beacons our way through the labyrinth of life. Often, life's challenges can seem overwhelming, escalating into cyclones of despair that threaten to uproot our faith. Despite these tempests, we are not left without an anchor. The bible, in its profound wisdom and timeless truths, provides us with a spiritual toolbox with which we can endure.

Drawing from lessons that are both admonishing and comforting, we can devise strategies to overcome and thrive, even when we find ourselves in the eye of the storm.

First and foremost, prayer stands as a formidable tool. The potent dialogue between the divine and the believer, prayer offers an outlet for our fears, a platform for gratitude, and a source of strength in times of turmoil. Philippians 4:6 shows us how: "Do not be anxious about anything, but in every situation, by prayer and petition, with thanksgiving, present your requests to God."

Next, the Word of God serves as an arsenal of wisdom, guidance, and hope. By praying, reading, and meditating on the scriptures, we engage in an intimate communion with the Lord, and in this closeness we can glean strength, comfort, and wisdom. As Psalm 119:105 declares, "Your word is a lamp for my feet, a light on my path."

Furthermore, faith is another invaluable tool in our spiritual arsenal. Hebrews 11:1 narrates, "Now faith is confidence in what we hope for and assurance about what we do not see." This assurance, birthed by faith, inspires resilience. It teaches us that there is a divine plan, greater than our understanding, and in this truth, we find the strength to press on.

Engaging in worship and fellowship serves to fortify our spiritual resilience. Worshipping God, even amid painful circumstances, brings us to a place of surrender. It's an encumbrance lifted and a faith reaffirmed. Moreover, fellowship with like-minded believers offers not just psychological but spiritual support. Community strengthens resolve and fuels hope when we may feel ours is dwindling.

Finally, the practice of service acts as a tool for endurance. Just as Jesus demonstrated throughout the New Testament, a lifestyle revolving around serving others can yield profound satisfaction and a sense of purpose. Even in the grip of our storms, diverting attention towards the welfare of others can induce a transformative shift in our perspective.

Navigating life's storms in contemporary society can seem daunting, but utilizing the Bible's spiritual toolbox equips us with shields of faith, wisdom, and resilience. Prayer, the Word of God, faith, worship, fellowship, and service, when exercised mindfully and consistently, are able to steer us through these rains with renewed peace and deeper spiritual strength. By harnessing these profound tools, we transform turbulence into calmness, testing into triumph, and remain steadfast in the tumultuous seas of life, upholding what 1 Corinthians 16:13 advises us: "Be on your guard; stand firm in the faith; be courageous; be strong.

Journal Exercise:

Begin by summarizing your key insights from the chapter '9.3 Future Directions for Study' in three brief statements. Reflect on the principles discussed, how they align with your current understanding of faith-based resilience and spiritual strength, and how they guide your future studies.

Next, choose one story from the Bible that has inspired you or changed the way you perceive resilience and faith. Describe why this story was impactful to you and how you plan on applying the principles learned into your day to day life.

Finally, write a real-life situation where resilience and spiritual strength can be enhanced by implementing the faith-oriented principles discussed in the chapter. Reflect on what potential challenges you might face and how you plan on overcoming them.

Disclaimer

The contents of this book, "Echoes of Hope: A Comprehensive Bible Study on Faith's Resilience - Delving Deep into Bible Stories for Modern Serenity and Spiritual Strength," are provided for informational and inspirational purposes only. The author, publisher, and contributors make no representations or warranties regarding the accuracy, completeness, or suitability of the information contained herein.

The Bible, as a religious and sacred text, carries profound significance and interpretations that may vary among individuals and religious denominations. This book's interpretations and insights into Bible stories are the author's personal perspective and may not necessarily reflect the views or teachings of any particular religious group or denomination.

Readers are encouraged to consult with their spiritual leaders, clergy, or religious authorities to seek guidance and discernment in matters of faith and spirituality. The author and publisher disclaim any liability for any direct or indirect consequences resulting from the use, interpretation, or application of the information presented in this book.

While every effort has been made to ensure the accuracy and reliability of the content, the author and publisher do not assume responsibility or liability for any errors, omissions, or inaccuracies. Readers are advised to cross-reference and verify the information presented here with their own religious texts, trusted sources, or spiritual advisors.

The experiences and testimonials shared in this book are the personal accounts of individuals and may not be applicable to all readers. Each person's faith journey is unique, and results may vary.

By reading this book, you acknowledge and agree to the terms of this disclaimer. It is essential to approach matters of faith and spirituality with an open heart, humility, and a commitment to seeking truth and understanding in accordance with your own beliefs and convictions.